Intelligent Thinking

Overcome Thinking Errors, Learn Advanced Techniques to Think Intelligently, Make Smarter Choices, and Become the Best Version of Yourself

Som Bathla

www.sombathla.com

Your Free Gift

As a token of my thanks for taking out time to read my book, I would like to offer you a free gift:

Click Below and Download your **Free Report**

Learn 5 Mental Shifts To Turbo-Charge Your Performance In Every Area Of Your Life - in Next 30 Days!

You can also grab your FREE GIFT Report through this below URL:

http://sombathla.com/mentalshifts

Table of Contents

Introduction

"The world we have created is a product of our thinking; it cannot be changed without changing our thinking."

~ Albert Einstein

It was year 2002. He had just sold his stakes in a high-tech online payment company that brought him a hefty multi-million dollar fortune in his early thirties. Despite attaining a huge success at such a young age, he didn't do it all just to enjoy sunning at beaches and doing nothing for the rest of his life.

This is Elon Musk, who had further crazy plans for his life and mankind. As a serial entrepreneur, his next move was to build something tangible in the real world that could change the world. Despite his past experience in internet business, now he was thinking beyond the earth and getting into the space business, with the objective of seeing the possibility of human life on other planets and even a human colony on Mars.

The next step was to find out how to travel in space – obviously through rocket technology. But the cheapest US rocket would have cost him no less than 65 million US dollars, and he needed a few of these to initiate research to see the possibility of life on Mars. In his search for affordable technology, he traveled to Russia and initiated discussions with a few rocket companies to explore buying rockets from them. But the cheapest rockets would still cost no less than 15-20 million US dollars each and that was even without any nukes. The crux of the matter was that even the hardest negotiations wouldn't have yielded him close to what he was looking for. He realized that he might end up spending everything he had made from the sale of his stakes in Paypal, without a clear sign of recovering it, if he went ahead with buying rockets from outside.

Had he been someone else, he might have become frustrated and just quit at such roadblocks, but not Musk. So what did he do? He thought differently. He started exploring whether he could make rockets by himself despite his lack of experience in a new domain that was entirely different from what he had done during entire life so far. The next step was to dig him deeper into learning what this space technology was all about and how it operated. It was definitely a mammoth task for any internet entrepreneur to even fathom the thought of cracking space technology, but Musk, after many failures and almost losing his entire life earnings, finally cracked the code, and today his company SpaceX is a preferred vendor for huge orders of space rockets from the United States government.

Can you imagine Musk's internal thinking process, when he was contemplating manufacturing rockets? In one interview, he explained how he thought about and looked at the problem of manufacturing rockets on his own[1]:

"I tend to approach things from a physics framework. And physics teaches you to **reason from first principles rather than by analogy**. So I said, OK, let's look at the first principles. What is a rocket made of? Aerospace-grade aluminum alloys, plus

---

[1] https://www.wired.com/2012/10/ff-elon-musk-qa/

some titanium, copper, and carbon fiber. And then I asked, what is the value of those materials on the commodity market? It turned out that the materials cost of a rocket was around 2 percent of the typical price— which is a crazy ratio for a large mechanical product."

Musk's first principle thinking was along the lines of the laws of physics – this means you need to first deconstruct the final product into its core ingredients and then see how differently you can work with these core constituents and produce something out of it. This kind of first principle thinking was used by history's great thinkers, including the ancient philosopher, Aristotle; but probably no one embodies the philosophy of first principle thinking at such a vast level more than Elon Musk.

Unfortunately, most people just see success as a series of "events", and they don't pay the required attention to the "process" that leads to the success– it involves sincere thinking at a granular level before you achieve the clarity of approach to reach your goals.

Investment legend, Warren Buffett, also gives credit for his entire success to developing the thinking abilities that enabled him to make the right investment decisions most of the time. He says, "I insist on a lot of time being spent, almost every day, to just sit and think. That is very uncommon in American business. I read and think. So I **do more reading and thinking**, and make less impulse decisions than most people in business. I do it because I like this kind of life."

The important question that arises here is what makes these high-achievers different from other people that puts them into an entirely different league – in a way that people start to see these people as super human? In fact, it is simply that they learn how to use an important human endowment- the human ability to think clearly and intelligently.

They know the pitfalls or flaws of older conditioned ways of thinking. They choose to disassociate themselves from the limitations of this thinking and make a conscious choice to read and learn the newer way, and thus they create different and unique outcomes for themselves.

They are strong believers in the natural principle, as stated by Stephen R. Covey, that everything is build twice – first in the mind and then in the real world. If you can learn to think better, your first creation of your mind is going to be of superior quality, and that will only lead to a high-quality second-level creation in the real world. To put it simply, your level of success can never be greater than your level of your thinking.

Everybody uses their thinking abilities quite differently, and the distinguishing factor between highly successful people and others who live a mediocre life is in their approach to thinking. Successful people use more of their minds and do so in a more effective way that supports in creating the results they want.

They are self-aware of their own thoughts and beliefs and know what is needed to enhance the quality of life and what sabotages growth. They work hard on getting their thinking clear before they can achieve massive success. As Steve Jobs rightly said, *"You have to work hard to get your thinking clean to make it simple. But it's worth it in the end because once you get there, you can move mountains."*

Let's try to understand this with the help of an example. Assume you are driving a car and you have to reach a destination pretty quickly. When you see a clear road, you will press the accelerator and increase the speed of your vehicle. Pretty obvious! But if you see someone learning to drive out of fear or maybe naivety put one foot on the accelerator and often put another on the brake despite the empty road, you already know what's going to happen. You won't reach your destination faster, and to the contrary, you will be damaging your vehicle by doing these contradictory activities. In their right minds, no one would do this to their vehicles. But, unfortunately, most people do the same thing in their inner worlds – their minds.

They try to learn and implement the best strategies and practices to achieve results – the equivalent of pressing the accelerator of our minds. But, unfortunately, they don't stand guard against the erroneous thinking patterns running through their minds due to an unsupportive environment and beliefs, which is equal to applying the brakes simultaneously while racing the car.

One of the important components of learning is to first unlearn before you learn anything new. If you realize that the old patterns of thinking don't further support and improve the quality of your decisions and your life, it's time to say goodbye to those thoughts. If you sincerely want to learn newer approaches, you can't keep clinging to past unsupportive modes of thinking and still learn a newer way.

This simple story of a rich man who reached out to a monk will help you understand the importance of unlearning for learning. The man was materially wealthy but lacked peace of mind, and this search led him to visit a monk. After reaching the monk, he started telling him what all he had read and his knowledge of various kinds of literature. Yet he still lacked mental peace and clarity of purpose in his life. The monk kept listening to him, and after few minutes, he offered the rich man some tea to get refreshed, to which the latter agreed. Now the monk handed over a cup and started slowly pouring tea in it from his kettle. As he was pouring the tea, the rich man shouted with surprise, "Hey, monk, what are you doing? The cup is already full and you are still pouring. You can't put any more into it."

Now the monk responded, "Your cup is also already full of so much knowledge, and until you empty your cup, I can't offer you anything new to learn. You have to create some space for the new material to come in."

Similarly, you too have to empty your cup to fill it with something new. You have to unlearn those past thinking errors that you will realize contradict the newer ways of thinking you are going to learn in this book.

For improving your quality of thinking, you have to follow a two-pronged approach. While you need to learn the best strategies to change your thinking for better, before that you have to become self-aware and get rid of unsupportive thinking patterns.

What You Should Expect From This Book?

You don't need to read this book any further, if you're sure about the errors in your thinking patterns and are already using more effective strategies to evaluate important life-situations and make better decisions. But if you feel that something is missing and you need guidance and better thinking models, this book will equip your mental tool box with some highly effective ways to help you think better, make better decisions and solve any problems.

Here is what you will learn from this book. You will understand the concept of how humans think in general. You will learn how you can change your thinking or beliefs regardless of your age. This book will cover the errors in your thinking patterns that are causing you unwanted stress and anxiety and leading to bad decisions. Once you are aware of the mental blocks that sabotage your progress, you will have more effective ways of thinking to make better choices. Lastly, I will cover how you can use your physiology to change your thinking and how some kinds of mental work are scientifically proven to enhance your cognitive abilities to a great extent.

So, let's get started.

Chapter 1: How Does Thinking Really Work?

****

"All thinking begins with wondering" ~ *Socrates*

This book is all about reprogramming your thinking and transforming you into an intelligent thinker. Therefore, before we address the issue, we need to understand the mechanism of thinking. Thus, the first question to be addressed is "how do we think?"

Let's follow the same approach that Musk took to understand how to build space rockets. Let's apply first principle thinking to the understanding of our thinking process.

Thinking takes place inside our brains and different portions are responsible for generating different actions in response to various stimuli. Therefore, first things first. Let's look at brain anatomy and understand the different portions of the brain.

Physical Structure of the brain:

In the 1960s, American psychologist and neuroscientist, Paul MacLean, invented the Triune Brain Model to explain the functioning of different parts of the brain in terms of its evolutionary process. According to this theory, three distinct brains have emerged successively during evolution and now co-inhabit in the human skull.

1. Reptilian (instinctual) brain
2. Mammalian or limbic (emotional) brain
3. Primate or neocortex (thinking) brain

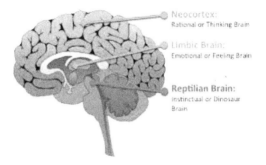

The reptilian and mammalian parts of the brain are very basic in nature and the oldest in terms of evolution.

The **reptilian system** of the brain is responsible for the most basic survival functions, such as heart rate, breathing, body temperature, and orientation in space.

This part of the brain handles all the body's involuntary functions and keeps you alive.

Also referred to as the "emotional brain", the **limbic system** is the reactive part of us that initiates the "fight or flight" response to danger. Our limbic brain contains the amygdala that primarily deals with anxiety, sadness and our response to fear. The amygdala helps safeguard us from danger and in fact helped us survive in the primitive age by prompting fight or flight reaction in difficult situations. Another important part of the brain is the hippocampus, which is like a scratchboard of our memories – whenever you learn and experience anything new, memories get coded in the hippocampus.

And the third part is the primate known as the **neocortex**. It's the "thinking" part of the brain, and you can also call it the "smart' brain" as it is the executive part of our system. The neocortex is focused on higher functions such as sensory perception, generation of motor commands, spatial reasoning, conscious thought, and, in humans, language. It's only this part of the brain that makes you distinct from animals, as it is responsible for human consciousness. The frontal lobe of your neocortex handles personality and reasoning, planning and executive functions. Most thinking happens in the front part of this frontal lobe called the **prefrontal cortex,** or the adult in your head.

The three various parts of the brain handle different tasks, but given modern safe environments (we don't live in jungles anymore), the role of the emotional brain is not often required; we don't feel the need for physical fight or flight in modern life as a rule. The reptilian brain will always be there to take care of our involuntary reactions (there is not much we need to do in that area) and the prime functions of our body like respiration, digestion, etc. that need to happen every moment of our lives.

Therefore, the most important part of the brain turns out to be the neocortex, which is responsible for success or failure, depending upon how you control it. The neocortex is literally the house of your thinking abilities, where you can either do nothing and let the older patterns dominate or you take control of this highly powerful human endowment and design your thinking to create the life for which you've always aspired.

Okay, we have talked briefly about the different portions of the human brain, which are physically visible as organs, and how thinking is closely related to our neocortex. Now let's keep moving on and try to understand the invisible thinking process.

Thinking: The Invisible Mental Process of Your Mind

You can physically see the head and by incision/surgery, you can also see inside it. The outside and inside are the physical and tangible portions that everybody recognizes. While the brain is physical organ that you can see, your mind is intangible, but you can experience the thoughts and emotions going on inside your mind and body.

The right analogy to understand the brain and mind interrelation is a comparison of the physical hardware of your computer versus the invisible software that operates the computer. The brain is your physical hardware. You can name the different portions of a laptop like the CPU, monitor, keyboard, etc. precisely in the same way that you define your brain in terms of the pre-frontal cortex, hippocampus, amygdala etc.

The software portion is the windows operating software (or any other operating software) that runs the different computer computations or commands in the background. Your mind is like the software in your brain that operates on the basis of commands that have been programmed in your machine by years of conditionings by your parents, teachers and society in general.

The chip in the computer equals the neurons we have in our brains. The complexity of the brain can be understood from the fact that we have more than 100 billion neurons in our heads. Learning from these neurons happens by way of their connection with one another. Each connection records some experience of learning. These connections are known as **synapses**. If we imagine all the stars in the Milky Way galaxy, there are more connections in our brains than all those stars combined. Surprisingly, a three-year-old child has 1000 trillion synapses blooming and pruning at the same time.

Every moment of your life, your neurons are constantly firing and building new connections. That is why when suddenly a thought comes to your mind, you let it go haywire in endless directions. For example, let's assume you attended a particular conference related to work and a memory infuses your brain. Immediately, you think about a person you met there, what this person's profession was, leading to another thought - where he used to work. Next you remember the street where his office is and then some famous street food joint where you had eaten something exciting in the past. That memory of eating something there then sends another message to your brain that creates a craving in your mind, and the next thing you do is move to the kitchen or refrigerator to fetch something to eat.

You see the sequence. It took me some time to type all these thoughts in words, but our brain acts at a super-fast pace and creates all these sequence in fractions of seconds. It's also important to note that we have two types of memories: working memory and long-term memory. While our long-term memory can store a wealth of information and has unlimited storage, on the other hand, our short-term working memory is really short term. We cannot handle more than 5-7 pieces of information at any one point of time. Whatever kind of thinking runs regularly in our brains, those neurons fire with each other and create a specific neuro-pattern or neuropaths, which will then go to our long-term memory and become part of our brains.

Therefore, unless we infuse a new kind of knowledge or environment into our lives on a regular basis, all our thinking will be nothing but the repetition of the same older thoughts. Studies show that the human mind runs around 60,000 thoughts on a daily basis and ironically more than 90-95% of them are the same and repetitive. So, you can understand how habitual our thinking is. In the later sections of this book, we will talk about ways to disrupt this pattern and adopt ways to bring novelty into our thinking process.

Thinking Vs. Thought

Thinking is active work and it's different from thoughts. Thoughts are passive. While reading this book, concentrating on what you are reading and internalizing it constitutes the active work of thinking. But at times, you might drift off. For example, you just heard your dog barking, or the sound of some vehicle passing by, and then you might suddenly start getting thoughts about going to the supermarket and buying something for tomorrow's breakfast. Or you might recall a road trip with friends or maybe your commute to the office. And suddenly, you realize that without any direct effort on your part, your thoughts have carried you away to many places. One thought leads to another, and if you don't interrupt this pattern, there will be a chain of endless thoughts.

Most people don't realize this, but allowing your mind to wander can lead to dozens or even hundreds of automatic thoughts and can cost much precious time. You can do an experiment on your own. Do it now. Let your mind wander for say a couple of minutes (a few minutes are enough, as thoughts travel pretty fast at fractions of seconds). Then suddenly, ask your mind to stop at any thought. Now you have to analyze your experiment. Start from the latest thoughts and keep asking yourself, "from where did this thought come?" Quickly write down a bullet point to record the origin of that thought. Don't stop - continue to repeat the same question again, "Where did this next thought come from?" Then write another bullet point. Write another quick bullet again. Repeat the process until you get to the first thought, where you allowed your mind to wander aimlessly.

How was the experiment? What did you realize?

I hope you had noticed that thoughts appear on their own without deliberate effort on your part, one after another. But when you try to recall these thoughts, it became thinking work in progress.

Thinking is always conscious. Letting yourself drift in your thoughts is always involuntary. Thinking puts you in the driver's seat whereas thoughts become the driver of your vehicle and can make you wander aimlessly. Your power lies in consciously controlling your thoughts and purposefully directing them toward what you want. If you don't control such thoughts, they control you. And what happens next. Our minds work on preset autopilot thinking patterns based on the memories recorded in the brain's neuropathways; and your uncontrolled thoughts often lead you to places where you didn't want to go.

Therefore, the first principle of intelligent thinking is to realize that thinking is an ACTIVE process and thoughts are all PASSIVE. And your job is to control your thinking. Although some form of passive thinking is good for you, that thinking model is not entirely passive, which is covered later in this section.

Intelligent Thinking Doesn't depend on your IQ

Now let's address one more myth that cripples many people to start thinking differently. They believe that thinking requires a greater Intelligence Quotient ((IQ) and a lack of IQ makes them less eligible to think intelligently.

Let's briefly look at the origin of IQ tests. The original IQ tests were developed in the early 1900s, and their main objective was to help predict which children were most likely to experience difficulty in school. An IQ was originally calculated by dividing mental age (measured by the test) by actual age, and multiplying the resulting quotient by 100. The resulting number is your IQ score, and it's compared to the rest of the population on a scale of 0–200.

While many tests have been developed since then, like the Wechsler Intelligence Scale for Children (WISC), the Stanford-Binet, Wechsler Adult Intelligence Scale Third Edition (WAIS--III), the Kaufman Assessment Battery for Children (KABC-II), etc., the major thing all IQ tests have in common is that they measure a person's cognitive ability—specifically **their ability to**

solve simple and theoretical problems
.

If you ever check out the highest ever IQs in the world, you won't recognize many names. But you'll also notice that many intelligent thinkers of the world didn't have that high an IQ. Albert Einstein and Stephen Hawking had an IQ of 160, which is consider good, but that's not as astronomical in proportion as compared to William James Sidis (an American mathematician, who had an IQ score of 250-300 or Tarence Tao, another mathematics genius (IQ score- 225- 230)[2].

Keith Stanovich, a professor of human development and applied psychology at the University of Toronto, Canada, and the author of *What Intelligence Tests Miss,* has stated[3] that *"IQ tests measure an important domain of cognitive functioning and they are moderately good at predicting academic and work success. But they are incomplete. They fall short of the full panoply of skills that would come under the rubric of 'good thinking'."* IQ isn't everything.

---

[2] https://www.scienceabc.com/humans/who-are-some-of-the-people-with-the-highest-iq.html
[3] https://som.yale.edu/news/2009/11/why-high-iq-doesnt-mean-youre-smart

"A high IQ is like height in a basketball player," says David Perkins, who studies thinking and reasoning skills at Harvard Graduate School of Education in Cambridge, Massachusetts. "It is very important, all other things being equal. But all other things aren't equal. There's a lot more to being a good basketball player than being tall, and there's a lot more to being a good thinker than having a high IQ."

Intelligent thinking does not entirely depend on IQ; rather it depends more on temperament and life-long learning, as Warren Buffett and his billionaire partner, Charlie Munger, believed. You can outsmart people who are smarter than you if you have two skills, as Buffett and Munger stated in one interview:

a. **Temperament** is more important than IQ. You can work with a reasonable intelligence, but you need to have the right temperament.

b. Secondly, you must be **committed to life-long learning**. Warren Buffet is much better in his 80's than he was at a young age, as Charlie Munger has pointed out. If you keep learning all the time, it adds up, and you have a wonderful advantage over others.

In the previous section, we have explored deeper into the layers of our minds to know the functioning of different layers of the brain. We examined the "active" thinking process compared with the "passive" thoughts coming in our heads. We also discussed how IQ is just one of the factor determining the thinking abilities of the human brain with lots of others that contribute to effective thinking. Before we conclude this chapter, let's understand the different types of thinking adopted by people.

Different Types of Thinking

There are different types of thinking ranging from the simplest form of perceptual thinking to complex critical and system thinking. The idea here is to give you some food for thought and to help you explore what kind of thinking you do mostly. This will also give you some perspective about how the people around you think in particular. I'm sure, while reading about these different types of thinking, you'll recall many persons around you and perhaps label them as a particular type. Let's get a brief understanding of the different types of thinking styles.

Perceptual Thinking

This the simplest form of thinking, where you perceive the things based on your own life experiences. It's also known as concrete thinking, as you only perceive things that you've actually experienced. This type of thinking only takes into account one's own perception of life, and it's entirely based on own life experiences. You can very well guess that this is a very limiting type of thinking or "in-the-box" thinking.

Conceptual or Abstract thinking

This is a superior version of thinking wherein you consider various other concepts, objects and languages, etc. Since you are thinking beyond your own limited perceptual world, this helps in understanding others' perspectives and the world in general. People with this type of thinking are open to exploring different ideas and do not just limit themselves to their own limited life experiences.

Reflective thinking

As the name suggests, this process of thinking involves a deep reflection of past experiences, and one's knowledge and skills. It is used for solving complex problems. In this process, you arrange your experiences about a particular situation, your skillset and all relevant facts related to the problem in a logical order and then reflect on the situation holistically. Reflective thinking is important to avoid hasty and impulse decisions and helps to give your best shot by taking full advantage of whatever knowledge, information, and skillset you possess. You feel confident about decisions made after reflective thinking.

Creative Thinking

This type of thinking involves looking out for new ideas and concepts based on your past learning and life experiences. It might be fusion of two existing ideas and the formulation of a new concept, or it could involve using sudden insights or sparks of intuition to enhance experimentation in the real-life situations. This type of thinking is possible for those who don't want to limit themselves to logics or reason. Creative thinking is vast and could entail wandering in any direction to acquire new ideas and thoughts. This is a superior form of thinking, where you are open to exploring and willing to listen to your intuition; thus the possibilities are limitless. That's why Einstein said, "Imagination is more important than knowledge. For knowledge is limited, whereas imagination embraces the entire world, stimulating progress, giving birth to evolution."

Critical Thinking

This mode of thinking is all about stepping aside from personal beliefs, presumptions, prejudices, and opinions to sort out your thoughts, discover truths and solve problems. This thinking requires a higher cognitive thinking skill.

Critical thinking is a higher order, well-disciplined thought process, which involves the use of cognitive skills like conceptualization, interpretation, analysis, synthesis and evaluation for arriving at a valid, unbiased judgment. A critical thinker examines any proposal through the lens of "what could go wrong with this proposal?" and then finds the arguments or solutions to address the challenges that could arise in future. Therefore critical thinking plays a "devil's advocate" role and therefore helps you take precautions when necessary.

Non-directed or Associative Thinking

We talked about allowing our minds to wander in any direction when we explained the difference between "thinking" and 'thoughts". Non-directed or associative thinking is such a free flow of thinking in an undirected manner. Here you give wings to your imagination and let it flow. This is non-directed, non-targeted mode of thinking, where you allow your mind to associate thoughts along different lines and allow building new-neuro-connections in your brain to trigger new possibilities.

There is a huge difference between aimless wanderers and associative thinkers. The aimless wanderer doesn't intend to derive any benefit from his thinking, whereas people using associative thinking do it purposefully to tap into the unconscious deeper thoughts etched in the long-term memories of our brains and then connect everything to bring creative solutions to any problems.

We covered a lot in this section about how we think. Now let's move on to the next section, where we will bust the common myths or misconceptions of people who believe that it is difficult to change one's thinking.

Chapter 2: Can You Really Change the Way You Think?

****

"There are no limits to what you can accomplish, except the limits you place on your own thinking."

~ Brian Tracy

So far we already learned about how human brain functions, how the neurons fire, connect and build specific neural pathways in our brain. Though, first we created these pathways through consistent behavior, later these oft-repeated thinking patterns hard-wired us to think in a specific way.

As we grow up, we become so integrated with our way of thinking that it seems almost impossible to think differently. But it's not that the way you have always thought will be the way you will continue to think forever. In fact, neuroscience has proven way beyond a doubt that our brains are malleable and can change, depending upon the circumstances and environment it is exposed to more often.

Neuroscience has proven the concept is neuroplasticity. Neuroplasticity is the ability of the brain to reorganize itself, both physically and functionally, throughout your life due to changes in your environment, behavior, thinking, and emotions. With the recent capability to visually "see" into the brain with the help of an MRI, science has confirmed the incredible morphing ability of the brain beyond any doubt. Our neurons have the ability to alter themselves chemically, structurally and even functionally and to optimize itself to the outside world, thanks to the concept of neuroplasticity.

In *The Brain That Changes Itself: Stories of Personal Triumph from the Frontiers of Brain Science*, author Norman Doidge states: "The brain is not an inanimate vessel that we fill; rather it is more like a living creature with an appetite, one that can grow and change itself with proper nourishment and exercise.

A new born baby is the most neuroplastic - he or she can be a warrior, musician, or a knowledge worker. That's why they say that a child is like a clean slate and you can write anything on that slate. Once a program is written on that child's slate, he or she continues to run his or her life based on the program, until the child realizes that he or she can choose a different program of choice.

Science has shown that neuroplastic changes keep happening during our entire lives, regardless of age or any other factor. Radical improvements in cognitive function—how we learn, think, perceive, and remember—are possible even in the elderly. Your brain makes physical changes based on the repetitive things you do and experiences you have. Now we can say that the quote by Jim Rohn has some scientific backing, "You are the average of the five people you spend most time with."

You can change the way you think by changing your surrounding environment, which include places, people or things. Your company influences your thinking.

Change Your Thinking regardless of Your Age

But still some people believe that after certain age it's really difficult to change or improve one's thinking. Many assume that mental and physical abilities necessarily decline with age and that we are, after age twenty-five, losing significant brain capacity on a daily basis.

But that's not the case. Again, studies and research have proven otherwise. **Actually, the average brain can improve with age**. Our neurons are capable of making increasingly complex new connections throughout our lives. And, our neuronal endowment is so great that, even if we lost a thousand brain cells every day for the rest of our lives, it would still be less than 1 percent of our total. (Of course, it's important not to lose the 1 percent that you actually use!)

You can literally start changing the respective portions of your brain, as per your own requirements. Our brains are so malleable that they do whatever it takes to help us achieve our purposes. Parts of our brains can increase with use or decrease if not used.

A study was conducted in London **on taxi and bus drivers** to check their brains. It showed that they had larger mid-posterior hippocampi (the portion responsible for memory) than average people. One taxi driver, he said, "It's almost like somehow somewhere up in your brain, and you've created enough space to slip this map [London street map] in, a little bit of software."

In research[4] done by Texas A&M neuroscientist, Bill Klemm, it subsequently suggested that new neurons are constantly being produced in our brains. And that's really good news for people who are getting old and fear mental decline. But the bad news is that these neurons must be continuously nurtured in order to survive. In other words, we either use them or lose them.

How Kids' Develop their Cognitive Abilities

When we plant a seed, it initially requires extra care and patience. You need to tender it well, water it properly, get rid of weeds, and give it proper manure. All this because you are setting the foundation and helping

------

[4] https://sharpbrains.com/blog/2008/04/25/new-neurons-good-news-bad-news/

the seed acquire deeper roots so to it can become stronger and grow faster.

The same principle applies to nurturing a kid. If you are a new parent, aspire to be or are teaching younger minds, you know the importance of nurturing the curiosity of a kid, making him or her aware about of outside environment and how to settle in this world.

What do we need to know to develop good thinking abilities in the next generation depending upon their cognitive abilities at a specific age? What are the learning capabilities of children at different stages of development? How do they develop their cognitive abilities?

French psychologist, Jean Plaget, in 1952 published his resourceful theory on cognitive development[5] in children depending on their age. His theory countered the prevailing belief of parents that children don't have the ability to think until they are old enough or have learned to speak. Plaget's research was about how children react to their environment. He

---

[5] https://www.learningrx.com/4-cognitive-stages-for-child-development-faq.htm

proposed four cognitive stages of development.

1. **Birth through about 2 years.** During this stage, children learn about the world through their senses and the manipulation of objects. It is called the **sensorimotor stage**.

2. **Ages 2 through 7.** During this stage, children develop memory and imagination. They are also able to understand things symbolically and to comprehend the ideas of past and future. He calls it the **preoperational stage**

3. **Ages 7 through 11.** During this stage, children become more aware of external events, as well as feelings other than their own. They become less egocentric and begin to understand that not everyone shares their thoughts, beliefs, or feelings. This stage is known as the **concrete operational stage**.

4. **Ages 11 and older.** During this stage, children are able to use logic to solve problems, view the world

around them, and plan for the future. It's known as the **formal operational stage**.

Children who are exposed to an environment conducive to new knowledge and learning tend to develop their cognitive abilities faster. Since their young and tender minds know nothing of the past, every new experience exposes them to new neuro-connnections over and over, which then forms part of their long-term memory and helps them to think better. Since children starts to understand and learn at much younger age, it's better to provide enough new learn materials depending upon their age and learning abilities. Since they understand a lot more stuff than we adults think, it's better to keep exposing them to new possibilities, making them visit new places, and meeting different types of people, so we can groom them faster.

Cognitive Self-Control Is More Important

In his book, "How Children Succeed", Paul Tough gives the example of a teacher, Elizabeth Spiegal, who had a specific way of training children. She believed that two of the most important executive functions of our brains are:

- **Cognitive flexibility**: It stands for the human ability to see alternative solutions and think outside of the box.
- **Cognitive self-control**: It means the ability of humans to inhibit an instinctive and habitual response to any situation and substitute it with a more effective and less obvious one.

Speigal's approach was that **it is difficult for human beings to focus on what they are doing wrong or badly**. She believed to acquire a new skill, you must be aware of exactly where you are going wrong. The first step to any change is self-awareness. Only after you have become aware of where you stand can you take the correct steps to move from that space.

The same applies to thinking. We are so closely associated with our thinking that seeing it from the outside and finding fault in it is very difficult for most of us. We learned in the first chapter how pushing hard on the accelerator and versus pumping the brakes won't make you reach your destination any faster. Rather, you are misusing your precious mental faculties. If you keep on making efforts to improve your thinking abilities, but don't take any steps to control the habitual impulsive thinking that leads to wrong choices, you can't go a long way.

The objective of this section is to explain that the concept of neuroplasticity gives us the assurance that humans can change the way they think, depending upon the environment and the circumstances they are exposed to over a longer period of time. There is the clear possibility that you can think the way you want to meet your specific objectives .

In the next chapter, let's talk about the most common thinking errors that trip us up, so we can start unlearning them before we master newer and intelligent ways to think.

Chapter 3: Most Common Thinking Errors You Must Get Rid Of

****

"Simple can be harder than complex: You have to work hard to get your thinking clean to make it simple. But it's worth it in the end because once you get there, you can move mountains."

~ Steve Jobs

Suppose you are traveling down a road. Would you think of stopping and changing the course of action unless you got some kind of hunch that you've inadvertently taken the wrong path? Would you even bother to explore another map until you know that you're going wrong or have an inclination to find some shorter or better way?

No, you won't. Because if you are convinced about the best roadmap to your destination, you'll never bother to look at the GPS, Rather, you'll simply keep on driving.

Same principles apply to life as well.

You don't want to stop and check the direction of your life unless you get some internal nudge or an inclination about something being wrong about your approach. The very first step to making any change is awareness about something that requires a change.

You chose to read a book about thinking better in an intelligent way. Does this mean that you don't think intelligently as of now? Please don't get offended. Since I don't know you personally, I can't make any assumptions about your objective of picking this book. Maybe you just want to test your knowledge of the concepts to understand if you are already intelligent, or you might need to still improve your acuity. Or maybe you think yourself as a genius and picked up the book out of intrigue to find out if there is something beyond your knowledge that it can offer.

At whatever stage of life you are, the point I am trying to impress upon you is that you can only change if you are convinced that there is something wrong with your current approach or you think there must be some better way.

Unless you see that there are flaws in your way of thinking, will you want to change? No, you won't. You may find it hard to believe, but you are so closely connected with your thoughts that you always think of them as right and therefore defend them. This is because you don't yet understand the other way, the better way of thinking.

Until Copernicus, a mathematician and astronomer of the 16th century, presented a theory that the sun is the center of the universe and around which the planets rotate, it was widely believed that the earth was flat and that the sun, moon, etc. rotate around it. Do you know the biggest disadvantage of that approach? No one dared to discover any other countries because they believed the earth to be flat and thought they might fall off if they went too far on the seas by ship or boat in search of other islands. Today, this thinking seems so funny, isn't it? But when the people of the

16th century corrected their view that the earth flat, the discovery of new countries started to happen.

Similarly, there was a concept of Germ Theory proposed in 1860s and 1870s by Louis Pasteur, a French microbiologist. Before the discovery and publication of Germ Theory, a huge number of mothers and newborn babies didn't survive during delivery due to the attending physicians. The doctors used to believe that the smell of blood and other factors caused this situation, so they put all their efforts into making the delivery rooms smell better by putting roses or other fragrances. But everything changed when Pasteur presented his thoughts on the lack of hygiene of the attending physicians and the use of unsterilized equipment that caused micro-organisms or germs to spread infections leading to a huge number of deaths. So a wrong way of thinking was primarily responsible for mass death. But as soon as the presence of germs was understood and the doctors started taking precautions to contain the spread of germs, the problem was immediately addressed and thus further loss of precious lives was halted.

The common phenomenon in both our examples is that until the prevailing thinking was disproved, people used to believe that whatever they traditionally thought was right, and hence they couldn't get desirable results. But the moment they became aware of their limiting views, it was like a laser-sharp ray of high-beam light immediately cleared their thinking and gave them major rewards in terms of discoveries, whether of new countries or saving precious lives.

Now let's understand why we think a particular way and continue to believe that our approach is right. Why don't we want to change our thinking, sometimes even after knowing that changing it can be much more rewarding? In this section, we will talk about the commonest reasons why we think the way we do.

Cognitive Bias

We have many biases towards thinking in a particular manner. This cognitive bias is known as the mother of all biases. Cognitive bias means we have a very strong tendency to justify whatever we believe is right. In fact, we are always on the lookout for evidence to justify whatever we believe as the truth. Instead of learning something new, we listen with a sense of urgency to prove our point as correct. That's why Warren Buffet once wisely said, *"What the human being is best at doing is interpreting all new information so that their prior conclusions remain intact."*

One of the world's best-known skeptics and critical thinkers, Michael Shermer, author of *The Believing Brain,* has explained the reasoning behind why we are so cautious about protecting our beliefs. He says:

"We form our beliefs for a variety of subjective, personal, emotional, and psychological reasons in the context of environments created by family, friends, colleagues, culture, and society at large; after forming our beliefs we then defend, justify, and rationalize them with a host of intellectual reasons, cogent arguments, and rational explanations. Beliefs come first, explanations for beliefs follow."

A psychological study was conducted with two groups of people: one in favor of the death penalty for deterring crime and the other against it. Both groups were provided with two detailed research papers on the effectiveness of the death penalty for deterring crime. One report established that the death penalty is effective, while the other concluded that it was not.

The results of the experiment showed that despite being aware of detailed scientific research and arguments and counter-arguments regarding the death penalty, each group became more convinced of the validity of their own position. People simply accepted the information that supported their pre-conceived notions and dismissed or neglected the conflicting information.

Why does this happen?

It is our tendency to subconsciously decide what we want to do before we even figure out why we want to do. We are naturally inclined to engage ourselves in the things we like rather than in the things we don't. Thus, we tend to find arguments for what we like and simply reject information that doesn't support these likings. Chip Heath, author of the book *Decisive,* aptly states:

"When people have the opportunity to collect information from the world, they are more likely to select information that supports their pre-existing attitudes, beliefs, and actions."

We Often Make Irrational (Emotional Decisions)

Though we tend to believe otherwise we make way more decisions influenced by our emotions than guided by logic or reason.

Nobel Prize winner and renowned psychologist, Daniel Kahneman, in his book *Thinking, Fast and Slow* explains that we have two different systems operating in our minds that control our thinking and decision making. Every time you have to solve some problem or make a decision, there is an interplay going on between these two systems, like two characters in a drama. These two characters of the mind are (1) the impulsive, automatic, and intuitive **system 1**; and (2) the thoughtful, deliberate, and calculative **system 2**.

System 1 operates intuitively and suddenly; it doesn't demand any conscious control of the mind. For example, if you hear a loud noise, you will suddenly jump and immediately your entire attention will shift toward the place from where the noise came. System 1 is part of our brain's evolutionary process; it was necessary in the primitive age for survival, where any sound or sudden reaction in our environment could be a matter of life or death. Any slight sound, such as the leaves of a tree, could mean a wild hungry animal will assault us in search of food. Although the sound might turn out to be the wind, it would be too risky to accept that so easily, so system 1 helped us survive in dire situations.

On the other hand, system 2 is responsible for executive decision-making, and thinking rationally and logically on some subject. System 2 deals with all the conscious activities of our minds that involve paying attention, controlling instincts, and focusing on the important work at hand— meaning all activities that require a deliberate focus of mind.

For example, if you suddenly get into an argument with your spouse, a friend or your manager, your instant reaction will come from system 1. You will react immediately based on an emotional pattern recorded in your memory about how you had interpreted the other person's behavior in the past. Your system 1 is prompt to react to any situation, and it will supply you with a set of reactions pre-programmed in your mind based on past experience. Thus, you might become angry or defensive with the other person.

However, if you apply your system 2 thinking, there might be genuine concern raised by the other person that needs to be addressed.

But why does system 1 often overpower system 2 in most situations? It's because system 1 runs automatically and system 2 is in a comfortable low-effort mode in the background. Also, there is the law of least effort, which reveals our innate mental laziness. Our minds tend to use the minimum amount of energy possible for each task. But referring a situation to system 2, which results in doing deliberate and conscious thinking, requires energy consumption. By contrast, system 1 wants to avoid that step to protect the mind's energy.

It's really not the optimal use of our minds to behave most often under the influence of system 1; rather, it's unfortunate to be guided by this mental laziness. Studies show that practicing system 2 tasks will increase focus and self-control and lead to higher intelligence scores. By being lazy and avoiding system 2 intelligence, our minds are limiting the strength of our intelligence.

Therefore, instead of always making impulse decisions based on the instant reactions of the mind, you need to slow down at times and use your analytical self to assess the situation properly. This way, you can avoid emotion-guided impulse decisions and make better and more rational choices.

Multiplying By Zero

Everyone understands that if we multiply any number, however big, it will end up becoming zero.

Can you find the answer to this complex mathematical equation?

$2,987,456 \times 3,987 \times 34 \times 0 = ?$

Of course, you will start looking at the numbers, but the moment you see a zero in a multiplication problem, a smile forms on your face. You now know that you don't need to solve this problem, because anything you multiply by zero will, however big the number, become zero.

We understand this in terms of mathematics, but this principle applies to our daily lives very much; yet we don't understand it and thus suffer a lot as a result. Let's understand this by way of an example. Assume you are trying to become the best basketball player and play for the best teams. You have following advantages also on your side:

a. a height of 6'8"
b. You are born and brought up in a city, which has the best competitive players in the world.
c. You have already won the toughest competitions in basketball championships in a very competitive game in your city.
d. And you've been selected to play for one of the best teams in the world, i.e., the Boston Celtics.

How does all this sound? Doesn't it look as if you have arrived and nothing can stop you from becoming the best player on the world? But, hang on for a moment. There is one more thing associated with all of the above. You are badly addicted to cocaine.

Now re-assess your situation given all the factual information above. What do you think are really your chances of becoming the best player in the world? In fact, the above scenario is not merely a fictional example; rather it's a real life story of Leonard "Len" Bias, a young basketball prodigy, who died due to a cocaine overdose after being selected to play for the Boston Celtics, a leading American basketball team.

The weak link of cocaine addiction nullified all the positive traits in an otherwise ultra-talented life. Unfortunately, we see our lives as a game of the "addition" of different factors, but life in many situations requires us to think in "multiplicative" systems.

Every life situation is not like a meal planned for a dinner party, where the variety of dishes served on the table works on the principles of the addition system. If one dish is not cooked well or spoiled during preparation, it doesn't ruin your party; your guests may still have a delicious dinner with all the other dishes.

But now take an example of a corporate or business life situation. Assuming you are a very talented person in some skill, are smart, have good qualifications and the relevant experience as well to excel in your field. But now add one more thing to this equation – you don't go along with the other colleagues in the office or fail at people management. What will happen? Simple, without the skill of people management, it's really hard to survive in a tough corporate environment.

When it comes to dealing with situations where a lot of things depend on each other and where the role played by one element curtails or speeds up the next process, it is a multiplicative system. You can't afford to have a single weak link in the system, or else all your best efforts will still derail you due to that one negative factor.

You can't run an Enterprise Resources Planning (ERP) system in any organization, unless all the parts and parcels work in synergy. ERP in any organization has to take into account all aspects from procurement of raw material, to inventory management, to production, to final delivery of the output products issuing invoices, and many more interconnected activities. If there is a problem in proper inventory recording, it will impact your invoices and ultimately will stop any sales or delivery to customers.

We can see the mathematical numbers clearly and determine where the zero is. We further understand that adding or reducing zero doesn't harm the figure at all, but multiplying any number by zero, whatever it is, will lead to make that number zero.

However, in life, although we understand what trait or aspect is zero, we often fail to determine whether the problem is an "addition" one or is it a "multiplication" problem. And this non-judgment about the type of problem is sometimes in itself the biggest problem. You can't solve a multiplication problem with a paradigm of thinking in terms of addition.

Loss Aversion

In the field of cognitive psychology and decision theory, the concept of loss aversion means that people are more concerned about avoiding loss, as compared to gaining something.

Psychologists have conducted studies that show that people prefer to completely avoid the possibility of loss rather than take a risk even if there is a chance of winning high. In fact, for most people, the pain of losing is twice as acute as the pleasure of winning.

We might think that our decisions are rational, clear and straight-forward, but that's a delusion – we often go for less logical routes when making decisions.

For instance, if you were to decide between gaining 100 dollars or avoid losing 100 dollars, you would want to avoid losing the money you already have. Per rational thinking, your happiness over a 100 dollar win should have the same intensity as your sorrow for a 100 dollar loss. But this is not the truth. The loss aversion cognitive bias tends to make the feeling of loss way deeper and more intense than the feeling of any gain.

Let's change the other example. Say you are asked to make a choice: you can win 120$ (with a high probability), but you might lose 100$. Even here, most people wouldn't want to take the risk, as the reward is not that high to compensate for the pain arising from the loss of 100 dollars.

Now let's make this offer a bit more lucrative. What if you were told that you can win 200 dollars and the downside is that you might lose 100 dollars only? Now there is a probability that some people will want to play the contest, as the reward could be double the amount of the loss, so once they are convinced about the gain being significantly higher, only then will they want to take the risk of losing something.

Take another real-life example. Marketing people use the loss aversion cognitive bias of customers to create a sense of loss in the minds of prospective buyers, so they can sell more of their products. They know that if they can convince you of a bigger advantage associated with buying within a limited time period, only then will you become ready to make a decision and part with your money. Because now you realize that by not taking action to buy something within a given time frame, you will be losing all the bonus items or bigger benefits that come along with your purchase. We regularly see offers like a festival weekend with heavy discounts from online retailers, which creates a sense of losing something if we don't buy during the limited 3-4 day shopping window. This loss aversion cognitive bias of the consumer helps sellers move more of their products by creating a sense of potential loss in their minds.

Anchoring

The anchoring effect is another cognitive bias, where you become influenced and rely too heavily on the first piece of information. After this first piece, if something else is presented to you, you weigh all the subsequent information under the strong influence of the first piece.

Take an example. You go to a store where they have set a limit of 10 purchases maximum per customer on your favorite package of cookies and buff it up with the words "limited stock" or until the stock lasts. Now it might be that you could lose only one or two packs, but this limit of 10 per customer does the work of anchoring you to a higher number. In this case you'll end up buying more packs of cookies than you really needed.

Take the example of TV infomercials. You'll noticed the familiar tactic when they start announcing the price of your favorite electronic gadget or home appliance by first quoting a figure of say $ 5000 and then giving you a different offer using the ploy of seasonal discounts or promotions. You can get that offer, not for $5000, but the lower $999. What happens here is they first try to convince you of the benefits of the product and anchor a value of $5000 in your mind, and when they reduce it to $999, you feel like you are getting a great deal.

In the marketing and sales world, the anchoring effect is used very frequently. Due to the initial anchoring of the higher price, the customer has already perceived the value of the product as $5000 and therefore buying at $999 appears to be the best decision. Also, since they combine the offer with a shorter timeline to grab it, they additionally combine the loss aversion bias with the anchoring bias, triggering you to make an instant buying decision. Just think about it and probably you will recall buying something influenced by this notorious anchoring effect.

However, assume they had directly offered you the product at $999. You might have started questioning this price or waited for a further discount. Probably, you would not have bought the product at this initial price.

Availability Heuristics:

The availability heuristic refers to a common mistake that our brains make by assuming that the instances or examples that come to mind easily are also the most important or prevalent. It shows that we make our decisions based on the recency of events. We often misjudge the frequency and magnitude of the events that have happened recently because of the limitations of our memories.

According to Harvard professor, Max Bazerman, managers conducting performance appraisals often fall victim to the availability heuristic. The recency of events highly influences a supervisor's opinion during performance appraisals. Managers give more weight to performance during the three months prior to the evaluation than to the previous nine months of the evaluation period because the recent instances dominate their memories.

The availability heuristics is influenced by the ease of recall or retrievability of information of some event. Ease of recall suggests that if something is more easily recalled in your memory, you think that it will occur with a high probability. A study by Karlsson, Loewenstein, and Ariely (2008) showed that people are more likely to purchase insurance to protect themselves after a natural disaster they have just experienced than they are to purchase insurance on this type of disaster before it happens. Their decisions are influenced by the recency of events and retrievability of information.

This approach distorts our understanding of the real risks. We often don't do the proper assessment of all the alternatives in front of us and are misguided by the ease of recall due to the recency of events or retrievability of information in our minds.

Experiencing Self vs. Remembering Self

Our minds don't remember experiences in a straightforward way, rather we have two memory selves: they are called the experiencing self and the remembering self, as Daniel Kahneman noted in his research.

We don't think and make our decisions based on real experiences, rather we make them based on our memories of those decisions. For example a full day enjoyed at an exotic resort can be remembered as a bad one, if at the end, you got into an argument with the resort manager over an over-charged bill or maybe due to someone spilling of coffee on you.

The experiencing-self deals with the past records about how we feel about the experience in the present moment. It asks the question, "How does it feel?" On the other hand, the remembering self does the job of recording the entire event after the fact. It asks the question, "How was it on the whole?"

The experiencing self is the "you" in the moment that lives through the event. The remembering self is the "you" who writes the history. But it is the remembering self that is consulted when planning the future, not the experiencing self. Hence, decisions are made based on the remembering self's construction of what has happened in the past.

But it is the experiencing self that gives the more accurate account of what happened, because our feelings during an experience are always the most accurate. The remembering self is less accurate, because it registers the memories after the situation is finished. However, the experiencing self and the remembering self don't agree on what happened, and, unfortunately, it is the remembering self that dominates our memories.

In one study[6], the subjects had a hand immersed in ice water at a temperature that caused moderate pain. They were told that there would be three trials. While a hand was in the water, the other used a keyboard

[6]http://journals.sagepub.com/doi/10.1111/j.1467-9280.1993.tb00589.x

to continuously record the level of pain. The first trial lasted 60 seconds. The second trial lasted 90 seconds; however, in the last 30 seconds, the water was slowly warmed by 1 degree (better, but still painful). For the third trial, the subjects were allowed to choose which of the first two trials was less disagreeable and repeat that one.

Here's what they found. 80% of the subjects who reported experiencing some decrease in their pain in the last 30 seconds of the second trial chose to repeat the 90-second experience! In other words, their remembering self elected the second option that required an additional 30 seconds of suffering.

The conclusion that comes out of this experiment is that the duration of an experiment does not count. It's only the peak (best or worst) moment and the end of the experience that gets registered in our memories, which forms the basis for future thinking and decision making

-----

In this section, we covered the most common thinking errors that can lead to bad choices. Simply becoming aware of these thinking errors will help you change your thinking patterns and thus your behavior. In subsequent chapters of this book, you'll learn the best strategies used by great thinkers in history and how you, too, can implement these strategies in your day-to-day life. Let's continue to the next section.

Chapter 4: Effective Thinking Techniques Successful People Use

"The whole of science is nothing more than a refinement of everyday thinking."

~ Albert Einstein

Thinking differently is nothing other than changing your sunglasses. It means that if you have put on dark brown shades, you'll see even a hot sunny day as a pleasant one. However, if you replace your glasses with a different pair, you'll see the outside world differently. Thinking is not something cast in iron in your brain that can't be changed. It's our belief about thinking that makes it so rigid such that it appears that we are structured internally in a particular way.

The pre-requisite to changing your thinking is to deepen your understanding that it's not any physical intrusion or incision in your brain or transplantation of a *"differently-*

thinking" organ – it's just like replacing your sunglasses that gives a better world view.

You'll realize that it's not the world that change; rather it's our personal worldview about different things that changes. It's our outlook and perspective that changes, as we start to see things through different lenses. The world is not as it is; it's the way we see it. Therefore, everybody has a different perspective and different opinions about things.

Therefore intelligent thinking is all about changing your sunglasses, or your paradigm of thinking and seeing the world. It's all about upgrading our worldview such that we see things with a different and more holistic perspective, allowing us to find better solutions to our problems.

What is the best way to think intelligently?

The best way to think intelligently is to think in mental models. Warren Buffett, the multi-billionaire investor and his billionaire partner, Charlie Munger, strongly advocate using mental models as an effective thinking strategy. They have successfully applied mental models to make high-stake investment decisions for billions of dollars in an intelligent manner to significantly enhance their net worth over their lifetimes.

Let's understand what the mental models are and how we can use them in our day-to-day lives. A mental model is the approach of mentally filing away a massive, but finite amount of fundamental, unchanging knowledge to form the tools that can be used to evaluate the infinite number of unique scenarios arising in the real world.

In a famous speech in the 1990s, Charlie Munger explained his approach to gaining practical wisdom through mental models in below words:

> ....the first rule is that you can't really know anything if you just remember isolated facts and try and bang 'em back. If the facts don't hang together on a latticework of theory, you don't have them in a usable form.
>
> You've got to have models in your head and you've got to array your experiences, both vicarious and direct, on a latticework of models. You may have noticed

students who just try to use recall and pound back what is remembered. Well, they fail in school and in life. You've got to hang experiences on a latticework of models in your head.

Well, the first rule is that you've got to have multiple models because if you just have one or two, the nature of human psychology is such that you'll stretch reality so that it fits your models, or at least you'll think it does....

The models have to come from multiple disciplines because all the wisdom of the world is not to be found in one little academic department. That's why poetry professors, by and large, are so unwise in a worldly sense. They don't have enough models in their heads. So you've got to have models across a fair array of disciplines.

Mental models serves like "cross-training for the mind." Instead of compartmentalizing ourselves in the small, limited areas we may have studied in school, we study a broadly useful set of knowledge about the world, which will serve us in all dimensions of life.

In a nutshell, a mental model is a way to enhance your cognitive apparatus in order to make more intelligent and strategic decisions. Take this interesting example from biologist Robert Sapolsky. He asks, "Why did the chicken cross the road?" Then, he seeks answers from different experts.

- If you ask an evolutionary biologist, they might say, "The chicken crossed the road because they saw a potential mate on the other side."

- If you ask a kinesiologist, they might say, "The chicken crossed the road because the muscles in the leg contracted and pulled the leg bone forward during each step."

- If you ask a neuroscientist, they might say, "The chicken crossed the road because the neurons in the chicken's brain fired and triggered the movement."

You will agree that none of these experts are wrong. They have their own perspectives of looking at things based on their life experiences and skillsets. Each individual has his or her own view of reality. But the challenges of life cannot be fully understood and addressed by one field. Someone rightly said: "If you give a small boy a hammer, and he will find that everything he encounters needs pounding."

All perspectives hold some truth. None of them contains the complete truth.

There are so many mental models that have been developed over the past decades and even centuries. As you might have noted, these come from different fields like mathematics, economics, philosophy, biology, human psychology and what not.

It's not humanly possible to learn all the mental models, and, in reality, it's not required to even learn all the models. If you learn only a few mental models from different streams, and start using them in your day-to-day life on a regular basis, you'll start thinking intelligently.

This section will talk about some of the important mental models that will help you view the outside world and things differently. They will equip you with newer, better and more holistic way of thinking to change your perspective about your life circumstances. Let's talk about a few of the important mental models regarding thinking.

Inversion Thinking

Everybody wants the best results for themselves in their chosen life pursuits?

- You want to succeed on your examinations with impressive grades.
- You want to launch new products that become successful immediately upon their launch.
- You want to get a promotion in your job to the next level.

All this sounds obvious, right? However, assume someone tells you to think the opposite of what you want in order to get what you want? It means asking yourself to fail on your exams, get demoted in your job, or sell products that fail on the date of launch.

Sounds too counter-intuitive, isn't it? Yes, it does. But there was a technique used by the famous Greek stoics. They suggested that if you really want something, ask yourself a question opposite to it and then figure out how to avoid that opposite outcome. This technique is called inversion thinking.

Take one of the above examples to understand this better. Let's ask how to get demoted or say even fired from your job? Now list out a few reasons why you could get fired:

- You don't co-operate or make relationship with your colleagues.
- You don't learn the job skills better and choose to use the old methods learned ages ago.
- You work as much as you are paid to do and are not willing to put extra efforts into delivering the required results.

You can list many more reasons for losing your job, depending upon your set of circumstances. Of course, I understand that you don't want to lose your job; rather, your objective is to get promoted faster.

Here is what the inversion thinking technique suggests. You need to avoid all the above reasons that could cost you your job. Generally, we are too focused on just the finishing line and tend to ignore or not pay the required attention to avoiding certain mistakes. Whatever our objective in life, a positive intention is a must to achieve the goal; but if you don't pay attention to the small things or pitfalls on the way, you'll unnecessarily add to your struggles that could be avoided otherwise.

Charlie Munger asks people, "What do you want to avoid?" and then counsels that success is overrated; avoiding failure matters more. He further goes on to state that avoiding mistakes is an under-appreciated way to achieve success. He once quoted the reasons for his success as avoiding mistakes in below words: *"It is remarkable how much long-term advantage people like us have gotten by trying to be consistently not stupid, instead of trying to be very intelligent."*

Inversion thinking is all about identifying the reasons that can lead to the worst case scenario and once you know them, your primary job is to avoid getting trapped by those factors.

First Principle Thinking

In the introduction of this book, you noticed how Elon Musk was able to create his space rocket company by using first principle thinking. First Principle thinking is one of the most effective strategies to break down the most complex problems into smaller solvable pieces that offers original and innovative solutions. It is an approach of looking at things the way a scientist would.

How does a scientist operate?

Scientists don't assume anything. They dig deeper and deeper into a problem, until they reach the fundament truth of the situation. What did Musk do? Musk went deeper and deeper into rocket technology and narrowed it down to the hardcore plain two fundamental elements, namely, the raw material or the components to manufacture the rocket and, secondly, the technology that propels and launches the rocket.

One of the biggest problems in implementing the first principle thinking is that most people think about the *form* of the stuff and forget the *functional* requirements. People think and talk in terms of analogies, and that limits the creative thinking process, because analogies create a wall that limits the free flow of ideas.

For example, until Henry Ford invented the four-wheel car, people could think of fast running *horses* only. Until the airplane concept was formed, people could only think *flying cars*. The problem here is that people know the existing form for carrying out a function, and, therefore, they simply want the next version of the same form, with better functional abilities.

It's only the people who talk about function and don't get too trapped in the form, who invite creativity in abundance and thus come out with new solutions. The people who think in terms of analogies only talk about continuous improvement over the previous form, while first principle thinkers speak of improving the quality of function itself.

Here is the difference between continuous improvements vs. first principle thinking:

- o Continuous improvement happens within the boundary set by first design.

- o First principle thinking requires you to abandon your allegiance to previous forms and put the function front and center.

Let's understand this with the help of an example of invention of rolling suitcases. In ancient Rome, the soldiers used leather bags to carry food and other items while traveling the countryside. At that time, they were using many vehicles with wheels like the chariot, wagon, etc. But no one ever thought about putting wheels below a suitcase. It was in 1970 only, when Barnard Sadow got this idea when he saw a laborer using a wheeled skid to carry some heavy machinery.

Before this invention, people never thought of rolling suitcases; everyone was just making basic improvements in the existing "form" only. Someone put some additional zips or pockets on a bag, while others tried to use different kinds of material to make it more robust.

First principle thinking allows you to think more in terms of the *function* to be served compared to the popular practice of carrying out small iterations in an existing *form*. Therefore, all the changes made in suitcases before 1970 were just some other form of improvement by putting zips, adding additional bags or improving the material. But Sadow used first principle thinking and focused on changing the function, which ultimately led to the current form of the wheeled suitcase.

Elon Musk started as an internet entrepreneur, where everything he set up was virtual in an online world. But then he took an extremely different tangent to the physical world of electric cars and then moved on to physical rockets to other planets even. In all his entrepreneurship ventures, he focused on improving functionalities and improving human life, instead of improving existing forms.

How can you use first principle thinking in your daily life? There are few prerequisites to using first principle thinking.

- Think always in terms of function or the ultimate objective to be achieved.
- Break down the problem into tiny pieces like any dependency on different people, the resources required to handle it, specific challenges to be addressed, etc.
- It requires deep learning about the fundamentals before you can come up with an original and innovative solution to your problem. Therefore, you need to deeply learn the fundamentals and master them.

The more you think from the first principle thinking, more creativity you will invite that will help you perform your functions better.

Second Order Thinking

Now let's talk about another great way of thinking used by the most intelligent thinkers. There are two different perspectives to understand thinking – (1) first order thinking and (2) Second order thinking. *First order thinking* is not to be confused with the *first principle thinking*, which we learned in the previous point.

First order thinkers look for things that are simple, easy and defendable. But, unfortunately, the whole ecosystem we live in is not that simple; rather, it's a complex permutation and combination of various factors and their interaction at any given point in time.

Second order thinkers go way beyond the simple and look outside extending different parameters. They go to second, third and subsequent levels of probable consequences and think deeper. Second order thinkers think in terms of interactions amongst various factors, with attention to time- and system-related aspects. They ask questions like: (a) What different factors or parameters are involved in the problem and the interaction amongst them; (b) What could be different possible consequences of taking a particular action and analyzing each consequence, and (c) how to use leverage to speed up the solutions.

Howard Marks in his book, "The Most Important Thing", explains the concept of **second-order thinking**, which he calls second-level thinking.

"First-level thinking is simplistic and superficial, and just about everyone can do it (a bad sign for anything involving an attempt at superiority). All the first-level thinker needs is an opinion about the future, as in 'The outlook for the company is favorable, meaning the stock will go up.' Second-level thinking is deep, complex and convoluted."

Charlie Munger, while explaining second order thinking says, "It's not supposed to be easy. Anyone who finds it easy is stupid."

The problem with first order thinkers is that they all think alike and come to the same conclusions as others do. But here is the thing. Extraordinary things come by becoming different. You can't achieve phenomenal results by doing what everybody else is doing in the crowd. You need to be different. But be mindful: you not only need to be different, but you need to be correct too. Blind divergence is not the way. You need to opt for smart divergence.

Howard Marks speaks about the necessity for **smart divergence.** He explains that the conventional behavior will always lead to either average good results or average bad results, so you will get average results along with everyone else as part of the masses.

But if you choose unconventional behavior, then merely choosing a different path doesn't mean that you'll be successful overnight. If the outcome of your efforts is favorable, you'll get above average favorable results, which will make you an overnight success. But if the outcome is unfavorable, you'll face below average unfavorable results that might lead to frustration, disappointment and humiliation.

Here is how the equation works:

	Conventional Behavior	Unconventional Behavior
Favorable outcomes	Average good results	**Above average** results
Unfavorable outcomes	Average bad results	**Below average** results

Undoubtedly, to be ultra-successful, you have to stand apart from the crowd. But before jumping into something entirely different, bear in mind that you need to be a good second-order thinker. As a second-order thinker, you need to take into account a lot of factors that will interplay when you choose to follow an unconventional behavior. You need to understand the role of different people and how your ecosystem will affect your decisions.

Remember the principle: you not only need to be different; rather you need to be correct also.

Deep Understanding of Simple Ideas

"If you can't explain it simply, you don't understand it well enough." ~ Albert Einstein

To improve you thinking abilities, you need to develop a rock-solid understanding of simple ideas. This simplest understanding will help you build the strongest foundation for your success. You should have real knowledge of the subject in a way you can explain to your seventy-year-old grandma in simple language. Today's world is filled with pretend knowledge. People use jargon and difficult terminology to explain stuff, but they lack real understanding of the subject.

Again, Charlie Munger, once explained the **difference between real knowledge and pretend knowledge** while speaking at a commencement to USC Law School in 2007:

"I frequently tell the apocryphal story about how Max Planck, after he won the Nobel Prize, went around Germany giving the same standard lecture on the new quantum mechanics.

Over time, his chauffeur memorized the lecture and said, *"Would you mind, Professor Planck, because it's so boring to stay in our routine, if I gave the lecture in Munich and you just sat in front wearing my chauffeur's hat?*" Planck said, "*Why not?*" And the chauffeur got up and gave this long lecture on quantum mechanics after which a physics professor stood up and asked a perfectly ghastly question. The speaker said, *"Well I'm surprised that in an advanced city like Munich I get such an elementary question. I'm going to ask my chauffeur to reply."*

Of course, you'd have amazed by the presence of mind this chauffeur displayed through his quick-wittedness in handling the situation. But the point here is to distinguish between real knowledge and pretend knowledge. This chauffeur didn't have deep and real knowledge of the subject; it was merely pretend knowledge that is only at the surface level.

How do you gain real knowledge and deep understanding of the subject?

Richard Feynman, an American physicist a Nobel laureate, devised one simple technique to help you to gain real knowledge of any subject, instead of merely filling you with surface-level knowledge. This technique, known as the Feynman technique coined after him, helps you develop an in-depth understanding of any concept. Basically, it is a targeted learning approach.

There are the *four steps* of Feynman Technique:

Step 1: Identify the concept

Take a sheet of paper and write the name of the concept you want to learn at the top of the page.

Step 2: Explain in plain language

Now, start explaining the concept in your own words as if you were asked to teach it to someone else. The most important thing to remember here is **not to use the technical jargon** you have read in your learning material. You have to explain the concept in plain, simple language.

Many people use jargon or terminology of the subject in their explanations to others, even when they don't understand the concepts very clearly. This is because using jargon conceals our misunderstanding from the people around us. Therefore, don't cheat yourself. The approach should be to use plain and simple language, as if you were teaching the concept to your seventy-year-old grandmother, who has no knowledge of the concept.

Step 3: Review the Gap

In this step, you need to review your explanation honestly. Here you will identify the areas where you didn't know something completely or where you feel your explanation was wavering or not clear. You have to stop and go back to the learning material or previous notes prepared for learning the concept.

Step 4: Re-organize and Summarize

Once you have clearly understood the missing concepts, you need to again explain those concepts in plain language. If there are still any areas in your explanation where you've used jargon, subject terminology or complex language, challenge yourself to rewrite these sections in simpler terms. Make sure your explanation can be understood by someone without the knowledge base you believe you already have.

The Feynman technique will help you learn anything faster by honestly identifying gaps in your understanding of any concept. The technique is useful for learning a new idea, understanding an existing idea better, or preparing yourself for discussions on any complex topic.

You can't understand anything deeply if you've cluttered and stocked all kinds of information in your head. You need to seek the essential and discard the rest. Be open and see what's there and what's missing.

Deeper understanding of anything requires some deep work. Cal Newport in his book, Deep Work, explains the concept of deep work and shallow work. Deep work consists of activities performed in a state of distraction-free concentration. It pushes your cognitive capabilities and:

- The outcome is rare
- The outcome has new value
- You improve your skill
- The outcome is hard to replicate

On the other hand, Shallow Work is non-cognitively demanding, has logistical-style tasks, and often performed while distracted. These efforts:

- Don't create any new value
- Are easy to replicate
- Are not rare

Thinking intelligently needs utmost clarity of different concepts. Once you have a deeper understanding of different topics, you stand to gain an edge over others, who are either specialized only in specific fields or have scattered knowledge of different things.

But Deep work requires deep recovery too

You can't continue to do deep work if you are not giving yourself the necessary time to recover and rejuvenate. You won't be able to learn and improve your skills if you continue to push yourself. Your mental muscles are like your physical muscles. If you've ever followed a training regime for a physical workout, most trainers don't force you to build your muscles all the time. A strenuous exercise regime has to be followed by a period of rest in order to build strong, smooth muscles.

The formula for growth is a combination of stress and recovery. The equation is like this:

Stress + Recovery = Growth

Jim Loehr, a performance psychologist, in his book *Toughness Training for Life* emphasizes the above formula in these words:

> It's important to understand that only rarely does the volume of stress defeat us; far more often the agent of defeat is an insufficient capacity for recovery after the stress. Great stress simply requires great recovery. Your goal in toughness, therefore, is to be able to spike powerful waves of stress followed by equally powerful troughs of recovery. So here is an essential Toughness Training Principle: **Work hard. Recover equally hard.**

From a training perspective, recovery should receive as much attention as stress. Unfortunately, this is rarely the case. He puts it this way: *"Precisely the stress is the stimulus for growth. Recovery is when you grow."*

Recovery Improves Your Production Capacity

I remember one example referred to by Stephen R. Covey in his book, *The 7 Habits of Highly Effective People* that is relevant here to emphasize this point. It is related to a manager at a manufacturing location of an organization. The organization imported new state-of-the-art heavy machinery with the capacity to produce quality products at a lesser price. This manager was responsible for large quantities of high-quality products in a relatively short span of time. He started with full utilization of the new machinery. He operated it 24/7 at maximum capacity. He paid the least attention to downtime, recovery breaks or the general maintenance of the machinery. As the machinery was new, it continued to produce results and, therefore, the organization's profitability soared and the manager was appreciated for his performance.

Now after some time, this manager was promoted and transferred to a different location. A new manager came in his place to be in charge of running the manufacturing location. But this manager realized that with heavy utilization and without any downtime for maintenance, a lot of the parts of the machinery had already significantly worn down needed to be replaced or repaired. The new manager had to put significant time and effort into repair and maintenance of the machines, which resulted in lower production and thus a loss of profits.

The earlier manager had only taken care of the goal of production and ignored the machinery, i.e., the production capacity, although he had short-term good results. But ultimately not giving attention to recovery and maintenance resulted in long-term adverse consequences from the running down of the machinery.

The moral of this story is that if you want to get high-quality work for a long time, schedule some time for recovery. Sometimes, sprints of longer work hours might be acceptable some days, but you need to compensate for lost hours by finding relaxation time.

Besides sleeping, recovery involves totally disconnecting from your work for some period during the day to let the mind process whatever it has consumed and experienced during deep work. Only if you give time to recovery will your mind literally etch your memory boards with the new learning. During this recovery period, you will get bursts of insight or intuition, which can be big aha moments.

Most senior executives often report that their best ideas come when they are relaxing or rejuvenating. You might also experience many "ideas-in-shower." Therefore, work on deepening your understanding of any subject to sharpen your thinking abilities, while at the same time nurture your mind and allow moments of serenity to present valuable insights to you during deep recovery periods.

Make Mistakes to Improve Your Thinking

"A man's mistakes are his portals of discovery." ~ James Joyce

People are so scared of committing a mistake, as if heaven would fall if they commit one. But this fear from committing mistakes is a major stumbling block to improving your thinking abilities.

In fact, mistakes are growth stimulators, because they indicate that you have taken some action even if that action didn't show the right result. It means you have closed one wrong door and now are open to something new.

Mistakes mean that you are shifting from taking an imaginary action and failing in your mind to real action on the ground through which you learn a real lesson in life. The problem of taking action in your mind is that you can't fathom how different uncertain and unknown factors will play out in reality. These real factors will show up only in real time in the physical world outside your mind. You can think in your head, but you can't act in your head. While thinking happens in the head, real action happens on real ground.

If you had a chance to read the first draft of this book or any other book, you'd declare the book as a mistake. The first draft of any book by any author always appears like a mistake, because it is nothing but stream-of-consciousness writing and putting ideas on the paper. In other words, the first draft is to just bring the author's creativity out of his head and onto paper. There still will remain many disjointed ideas and thought processes, which need to be fine-tuned; and many iterations happen during the second and third draft, when the author edits and solidifies a few points by giving the correct references and putting things in right sequence and flow.

But the fact of the matter is that the second draft wouldn't have been possible without the first draft. Therefore, if the author leaves the writing after the first draft, it would definitely look like a mistake, but it's only the first draft that leads to refinement and editing, and therefore creates the second and third draft of the book. After that, the editors and proofreaders play their roles in generating a final manuscript ready for the readers.

You can say that even a bestselling book is the result of making multiple revisions and rectifying numerous mistakes. Same is the case with the best music albums, the best movies, and the best theatre shows. The best TED Talks or speeches that leave people awe-inspired are the result of endless practice and learning from mistakes.

But here is the thing, the more you make mistakes, the more you'll learn as it will change your neuro-circuitry based on experience. Thomas A Edison once said, "I have not failed. I've just found 10,000 ways that won't work."

It's not merely philosophical advice to learn from mistakes; neuroscience has established that our brains are self-aware when they commit a mistake. As reported in an article[7],

[7] https://www.livescience.com/7312-study-reveals-learn-mistakes.html

Andy Wills, a psychologist at the University of Exeter and his team conducted research on a group of volunteers to test how their brains registered mistakes and learned to correct them. In the research, the participants were required to make predictions about the answers to a few questions on a computer screen. Once they made their predictions, they were shown another screen that illustrated many of those predictions as incorrect. The objective the research was to see how the human brain reacts when it realizes its mistakes. The study proved that as soon as the participants looked at the second screen, their minds realized the mistakes in fractions of seconds. The lower portion of the brain immediately sends signal to the whole brain about the mistake in milliseconds so that the mind doesn't commit the same mistake in the second round.

This study showed that the human minds registers mistakes quickly, even before it reaches the conscious thinking portions of the brain. It shows that the mind has the capacity to quickly learn from mistakes and register them in memory.

Committing mistakes at least moves your forward from your current situation to the next level. You either achieve results or come to know the faults in your approach. You gain both ways. Either you achieve your goals or else you learn the right ways to do it.

Now, let's move to the next section, where we will learn more strategies to improve your thinking skills.

Chapter 5: Additional Techniques to Activate Your Thinking Muscles

****

"Intelligence is dangerous. Intelligence means you will start thinking on your own; you will start looking around on your own. You will not believe in the scriptures; you will believe only in your own experience."

~ Osho

Let's continue to look at some more effective strategies to think intelligently.

Integrative Thinking

Every individual thinks differently depending upon his or her upbringing, the regular day- to-day environment and one's life circumstances. Each of us has a different perspective about life, and we view the things around us from that perspective.

In his book, *Opposable Minds: Winning through Integrative Thinking*, author Roger Martin explains a new aspect of thinking that he developed in 1986 known as integrative thinking. He defines integrative thinking as "The ability to face constructively the tension of opposing ideas and, instead of choosing one at the expense of the other, generate a creative resolution of the tension in the form of a new idea that contains elements of the opposing ideas but is superior to each."

Let's understand the concept of integrative thinking with help of an example of exploring how marketing people and engineers think differently. Marketing people keep an eye on market developments, carefully watching their competitors' moves continuously on the lookout for new marketing strategies to promote their products better. Through this approach, they consistently keep comparing the new inputs with their existing thought processes. But they are not able to effectively connect one piece of information with another nor the interplay of these different sets of inputs. In a way, they are shallow thinkers.

Engineers, however, have a more scientific approach to thinking and observing things. They keep going deeper and deeper to find consistent patterns between different pieces of information. They are more interested in establishing a cause and effect relationship. In a way, they are deep thinkers.

Now if these two sets of people sit together, each will be observing the problem in a different way. The unique way each sees the problem means that the marketing people will be filled with a broad range of information in their heads, but they will not be good at exactly pinpointing the relationship amongst the different factors. On the other hand, the engineers will be deeply focused on a few limited aspects, and their study of the subject will be intense. Now if you combine these two types of thinkers and let them brainstorm ideas, taking each other's perspective, it would produce the fruits of integrative thinking. They may come out with something unique due to the germination taking place within two contrasting approaches of observing things.

Integrative thinking is an approach to solving complex and tangled problems.

Roger Martin continues to explain integrative thinking in these words: **"Integrative thinkers *build* models rather than *choose* between them.** Their models include consideration of numerous variables — customers, employees, competitors, capabilities, cost structures, industry evolution, and regulatory environment — not just a subset of the above. Their models capture the complicated, multi-faceted and multidirectional causal relationships between the key variables in any problem. Integrative thinkers consider the problem as a whole, rather than breaking it down and farming out the parts. Finally, they creatively resolve tensions without making costly trade-offs, turning challenges into opportunities."

The reason that a lot of engineers prefer to have a Master's degree in business administration is so that they can combine their deep thinking abilities as engineers with vast business management skills.

Here's what Justin Musk (Elon Musk's ex-wife) stated on how idea fusion can put you on an altogether different trajectory of growth: *"Choose one thing and become a master of it. Choose a second thing and become a master of that. When you become a master of two worlds (say, engineering and business), you can bring them together in a way that will a) introduce hot ideas to each other, so they can have idea sex and make idea babies that no one has seen before and b) create a competitive advantage because you can move between worlds, speak both languages, connect the tribes, mash the elements to spark fresh creative insight until you wake up with the epiphany that changes your life."*

How to use integrative thinking

Next time you come across two different ideas, don't force yourself to choose one. While the separate ideas can be compared to commodities available everywhere, the combination or interaction between two different ideas can become a "brand" and a unique selling proposition (USP).

Remember the experiment where Barnard Sadow looked at two different ideas – one of using wheeled carts to carry heavy machinery and the other of heavy suitcases. Until then, no one had thought of integrating these two ideas, i.e., putting wheels on suitcases. Sadow used integrative thinking and created the idea of rolling suitcases, and it was an instant success.

Another example comes from Sylvan Goldman, an American businessman and inventor of the shopping cart, who came up with something different that no one else had thought of before 1937. He observed that in stores, people buy only as many grocery items as they can hold their hands. Once they are not able to hold more products, they don't buy further. Here is what he did. He took one chair, put wheels under it and then put a basket on the seat. This was the birth of the shopping cart, now a universal phenomenon. It's a great example of integrative thinking.

Integrative thinking brings a blue ocean of endless possibilities and can make you an instant leader in your domain, because while people are selling singular ideas, you used your thinking skills to effectively combine two different ideas and generate a new and unique one. And so you become the market leader.

Cartesian Doubt Method

René Descartes, a French philosopher of the 1600s, used to always doubt his beliefs, ideas, thoughts, and the world of matter. He showed that his grounds for reasoning and any knowledge derived from it could just as well be false. In his view, the sensory experience, for him the primary mode of knowledge, was often erroneous and therefore must be doubted. In essence, what one sees may very well be a hallucination.

Descartes' attempt to apply the method of doubt to his own existence spawned the proof imbedded in his famous saying, "I think, therefore I am." It means that he tried to doubt his own existence, but found that even in his doubting, he existed since he could not doubt if he did not exist[8].

Descartes developed a principle wherein you systematically doubt everything you could possibly see or do until you are left with an indubitable truth, a method known as Cartesian Doubt or Cartesian Skepticism. It is a systematic process of being skeptical about or doubting the truth of one's beliefs. This approach works on the principle of critical thinking.

When you start doubting your own thinking, beliefs and opinions and want to ascertain if

[8] https://en.wikipedia.org/wiki/Cartesian_doubt

they are true or false, you are taking the first step towards self-awareness. You can change something only when you're aware of it and are convinced that it needs to be changed. Only when you find that your beliefs are not correct will you take steps to find what is reality for you.

How do you use this practically in your life?

Take an example of any two persons in your life, one you love very much and another you hate a lot – symbolizing two extreme types of emotions. You must have some reasons or feelings that make you love or hate these people.

Now you have to start asking the question of why you love or hate a person and keep doubting it until you reach to a factual conclusion that can't be further doubted. It's like peeling an onion; once you have gone through multiple layers, what will be left will be the hard core truth. You should compare your feelings before this exercise and after it. Then you'll definitely find some change in your thinking and approach towards these loved or hated persons. There is a similar principle called the principle of 7-Whys, which requires you to keep digging deeper to find the core reasons or motivations behind your actions or beliefs. The idea is to keep doubting and questioning until you get to the deeper roots of the problem. This way, you prime your mind to seek answers to your questions from the deepest level of intelligence.

Kill Multi-tasking to Improve Your Thinking Abilities

People think that more they are able to handle a variety of tasks together, the smarter they are. In fact, our society rewards people who appear to be juggling different tasks at the same time. But unfortunately, multi-tasking is something that doesn't help improve your thinking abilities.

In fact, thinking is a slow and deliberate process that requires concentration, and it's a rather slow process. You can't multi-task and simultaneously think effectively. Multi-tasking not only means that you are not thinking, but that you are actually reducing your thinking abilities.

Thinking means concentrating on one thing for a long to form an idea about it. It means you are trying to extract different memories formed by your experience, firing neurons related to make new connections, and simultaneously using your imagination to create new solutions to the same problems. Thinking means developing new ideas.

Spend time concentrating and sticking to the questions, be patient, make associations, and draw connections between different ideas you have learned, and you can enjoy original thinking.

Multi-tasking fails at the basic level of thinking. A study[9] by Stanford University shows that regular multi-tasking makes it difficult for people to focus on one single task for a long time, but, more importantly, they find it hard to distinguish between relevant and irrelevant information. The multi-tasking participants in the study were worse in mental filing, which means they were not able to compartmentalize the information in their respective boxes to be able to retrieve it quickly when needed.

Therefore, not only does multi-tasking make people less effective, but when not multi-tasking, they are also less effective in prioritizing to achieve their goals.

In another study[10] at University College London, a neuroscientist conducted a study

---

[9] https://www.ncbi.nlm.nih.gov/pubmed/26223469

of the brains of frequent multi-taskers. They discovered a lower density of gray material in their cortexes, which resulted in observed decreased cognitive performance. One article showed that sitting near someone who does multitasking drops your intelligence by seventeen percent.

William Deresiewicz, author of Excellent Sheep and a literary critic, explains how thinking works. He says, "it's only by concentrating, sticking to the question, being patient, letting all parts of my mind come into play, that I arrive at an original idea. By giving my brain a chance to make associations, draw connections, take me by surprise."

100 Questions Technique

The quality of your life depends on the quality of the questions you ask yourself. Great minds ask questions. If you don't question, it means you're okay with the status quo; it means you don't want to grow. You can stop questioning only when you have reached the highest realm of growth – before that, you won't.

10

https://www.ncbi.nlm.nih.gov/pmc/articles/PMC4174517/

Leonardo Da Vinci, the genius Renaissance thinker developed this wonderful technique known as 100 questions technique. If you read a lot of books or are willing to spend your time learning new skills or growing in any field, there are a lot of questions you still have to answer. The 100 question technique is a deep probe into whatever is hanging around in your head and then choosing the real questions that matter most to your life. It will help you get clarity about your top priorities.

Here is how this technique works.

Step 1:

Give yourself a solid 45 to 60 minutes of time, when you won't get distracted. Sit comfortably and get your journal or any notebook. You may use your computer as well, but it's better if you write by hand if you want to use your senses in a natural way. Technology helps a lot, but here we are into an exploration of our inner world, so let's make use of the technology that the supreme power has provided to us - our hands.

It's comparatively better if you choose early morning for this exercise, as your mind is fresh and full of ideas. Now set your time for 45 to 60 minutes and start writing questions--any that come to mind about your life, your surroundings or anything else. Remember that you have to write 100 questions straight in this designated period.

While an initial twenty to thirty questions might come easily to you, it gets challenging thereafter. You'll feel dried up and think there are no more questions, but don't stop here. You have to keep asking yourself, "what else?" and keep writing your questions. If nothing comes specifically to you, you can write simple questions like "why roads are made with concrete and tar?" or "why do you like a particular food item?" or "what was the best thing you learned from your father."

You see, I'm giving you some ideas to pique your curiosity. While doing this exercise, you'll realize that in the initial twenty minutes or so, you will be generally writing. But in the later part of your time slot, you'll see some specific themes emerging. These themes could be around money, relationships, spirituality, personal growth, fun/adventure or anything at all.

For example, when I did my 100 questions, my themes revolved around going on adventures, exploring life, places and people, learning new things and testing the limitlessness of human potential.

The point is that you have to keep writing those 100 questions and not stop until you finish.

Step 2

For the next step, give yourself 20 to 30 minutes more. Now review all 100 questions you've written and let them spin in your head for a few moments. Some questions will seem absurd and non-important while a few others will appear to come from your genuine innate curiosity. These latter set of questions can be your life questions.

Now, you've to introspect and choose your top 10 questions out of the 100 questions. There can't be any right or wrong questions. These are the 10 questions you find most important for you and your life. You sit in silent, in an undistracted environment, and let these questions pop up on their own in your mind through your infinite intelligence. They are not superimposed by others. Of course, many out of the 100 questions may come out of your conditioned mind, but when you limit your questions to just the top 10, then you can't be misled by others. These questions will serve as your north star and will guide you towards what you truly want to find answers about. In your quest to find answers to those questions, you'll have immense clarity in your thinking process.

When you trash 90 questions, you are trashing all non-essential things and choosing to give importance to only 10 questions; thus this will improve clarity and focus and you can think more clearly.

This technique is very helpful because it gets everything out of your head onto paper using whatever is stored there already and also by squeezing everything from your imagination. In the next step, you get to know your top 10 priorities. This whole exercise primes your brain to be clear about what's most important to you; and with this clarity, your mind becomes focused and produces the ideas or thoughts that will serve your most important goals. As Tony Robbins wisely says, "Where focus goes energy flows."

Getting your top 10 questions is the act of finding your ultimate purpose. By the time you shortlist these questions, you will already have a sense of innate clarity in your mind see that your energy automatically starts flowing to where your focus has shifted.

Use Fluid Intelligence and Crystallized Intelligence

Researchers talk about another perspective which states that humans have fluid and crystallized intelligence. Understanding and effectively using these two types of intelligence will enhance your thinking abilities.

Intelligence is way more that merely a collection of a variety of facts; it encompasses the ability to learn new things as well. Psychologist, Raymond Cattell[11], first introduced the concepts of fluid and crystallized intelligence and further developed his theory with one of his students, John Horn.

The Cattell-Horn theory of fluid and crystallized intelligence suggests that

[11] https://www.verywellmind.com/fluid-intelligence-vs-crystallized-intelligence-2795004

intelligence is composed of different abilities that interact and work together to produce overall individual intelligence.

Fluid intelligence is often defined as the global capacity to learn, the ability to learn new things and the capacity to reason. On the other hand, crystallized intelligence comes from our prior learning and past experiences.

Fluid intelligence primarily is responsible for our ability to think and reason abstractly and solve problems. To put it simply, fluid intelligence refers to the ability to reason and solve problems independently of previously acquired knowledge. It's most commonly used in solving puzzles and coming up with problem solving strategies. Crystallized intelligence is handy when you have to take an examination or with your reading comprehension.

You ask which one is better. And the answer is both are important. In fact, both these types of intelligence complement each other. Cattell suggested that when both are combined, we get what we call general intelligence.

For example, if you are required to solve a problem, say, making a decision between leasing car versus buying a new car, you can think better and make a quality decision by using both types of decision making. Crystallized intelligence will help you use your previous knowledge and understanding of interest rates or other information that will help you get clear on the facts. But fluid intelligence will help you open up and explore the newer possibilities of considering your purpose in getting a car. You can take any simple to complex example from your family, work or personal life and use both types of intelligence to get the full benefit of your existing knowledge and experience (crystallized intelligence) as well deeply thinking, making new connections in your brain and solving your problem (fluid intelligence).

In fact, you can't separate both these forms of intelligence. The more you use fluid intelligence, think and explore, the better the newer information gets transferred to your long- term memory and thus becomes part of crystallized intelligence.

Crystallized intelligence can be improved through openness to learning. Since crystallized intelligence is all about long-term memory, the more accumulated knowledge you have, the more crystallized intelligence you will possess. Therefore, anyone can improve their crystallized intelligence by continuously exploring and learning new things through formal or informational education resources.

Previous research on intelligence suggested that people really don't have much control over their intelligence at all. It was believed that our IQ is largely determined by genetics and that training programs aimed at increasingly have limited effectiveness. A 2008 study[12], however, found that it is possible to improve fluid intelligence with brain training that focuses on working memory. Whereas long-term memory is focused on storing facts and information over long periods of time, working memory is a form of short-term memory centered on what you are currently thinking about. This type of memory involves not only storing information for a brief period of time, but also the ability to mentally manipulate that information.

---

[12] http://www.pnas.org/content/105/19/6829

Recent research on the ability to increase fluid intelligence by improving working memory has a number of important implications.

- Fluid intelligence can be trained.

- The more you train, the better your results.

- Skills are transferable to other domains; training in one area of working memory resulted in gains in other cognitive skills unrelated to the training tasks.

The latest research evidence indicates that you can develop a better brain by synthesizing properly both fluid intelligence and crystallized intelligence. With a developed form of intelligence, you will be able to think better and in more intelligent way.

Leonardo Da Vinci's 7 Principles to Thinking Genius

If you love to explore about ways to optimize and harness the minds' power more fully, you might consider the theories of Leonardo Da Vinci. He was a true genius and a Renaissance man of the fifteenth century. A

Renaissance man is a person whose expertise covers a significant number of subjects in variety of fields. Da Vinci was a painter, architect, inventor and a student with curiosity and a goal of life-long learning.

It's important to take a note of research conducted by Howard Gardner, a psychologist and professor at Harvard University, who concluded in his book that there are seven different types of intelligences:

1. Logical-mathematical— This kind of intelligence helps people do the things that require logic, abstraction, reasoning, numbers and more critical thinking. A few examples of people enriched with this type of intelligence are Stephen Hawking, Isaac Newton, Marie Curie.

2. Verbal-linguistic—People with high verbal-linguistic intelligence show great expertise in the field of words and language. Think William Shakespeare, Emily Dickinson, and Jorge Luis Borges as perfect examples.

3. Spatial-mechanical—This intelligence makes people good at visualizing very vividly through their mind's eye, providing them with the mental skill to solve spatial problems of navigation, better visualization of objects from different angles and positions in space, stronger facial or scene recognition, and an enhanced ability to notice fine details. Examples of this intelligence are Michelangelo, Georgia O'Keeffe, and Buckminster Fuller.

4. Musical— This area has to do with sensitivity to sounds, rhythms, tones, and music. People with a high musical intelligence normally have good pitch and may even have absolute pitch. They are able to sing, play musical instruments, and compose music. Mozart, George Gershwin, Ella Fitzgerald can be cited as good examples of this type of intelligence.

5. Bodily-kinesthetic—This type of intelligence allows the ability to control body movements and a capacity to handle the things very

skillfully. It includes a sense of timing, a clear sense of physical action, along with the ability to train one's responses. One perfect example of this is Muhammad Ali.

6. Interpersonal-social—People possessing high interpersonal skills are characterized by a sensitivity to others' moods, feelings, temperaments, and motivations, and an ability to cooperate in order to work as part of a group. Good examples of this intelligence are Nelson Mandela and Mahatma Gandhi.

7. Intrapersonal (self-knowledge)— People with this capacity can do much better at introspection and self-reflection. They have a deep understanding of themselves, their strengths and weaknesses. They know what makes them unique and are able to predict their own reactions and emotions. Viktor Frankl, Thich Nhat Hanh, and Mother Teresa can be given as perfect examples for this category of intelligence.

Leonardo Da Vinci was proficient in all seven areas of Intelligences. Michael Gelb in his bestselling book, Think Like Leonardo Da Vinci, explains that Leonardo had seven principles that led him to become a genius thinker.

Here are the seven principles Leonardo followed in his lifetime:

1. **Curious approach**: He had an insatiably curious approach to life and an unrelenting quest for continuous learning. He continued to enliven his curiosity by asking "what if" and "how come" to any scenarios he could think of. The question "what if" continues to provoke your imagination and "how come" makes you find the reasons behind everything. Gelb suggests that if you write down the ideas that come to you at four in the morning by recording them, you are inviting your intuitive mind to be more a part of your everyday thinking.

2. **Commitment to test knowledge**: He lived his life with a deep commitment to testing knowledge

through experience, persistence, and a willingness to learn from his mistakes. This principle requires you not to take anything for granted. Rather, you should test every idea and experience life first hand. You need to play "devil's advocate" to counter your own beliefs about different aspects your life. He believed that you should declare anything as true or false based on personal experience.

3. **Continuous refinement**: He believed in the continual refinement of the senses, especially sight, as the means to clarify experience. In his words, "The five senses are the ministers of the soul." Da Vinci was a strong proponent of exposing all senses to different experience be it smelling, seeing, touching, listening, tasting, etc. He was incredibly inspired by the world around him, and the more he honed his senses, the more heightened his genius became. He believed that sharpening the senses of sight, sound, smell, touch and taste are the keys to opening the doors of experience.

4. **Embrace ambiguity**: A willingness to embrace ambiguity, paradox, and uncertainty is the key life principle of Da Vinci. He had a very unique ability to understand the extreme opposites of opinions and phenomenon. He was also able to explore unknowns and revel in uncertainty. Most of us are uncomfortable with not knowing something or unanswerable questions, so we avoid anything out of our control.

5. **Balance between science and art**: He strongly advocated the principle of the balance between science and art, logic and imagination or "whole-brain thinking." Most people don't use both the left and right sides of the brain. Left-brain people think in words, use linear thinking, and are all about facts and logics etc. Other people who are right-brained are imaginative, think in imagery, and are more about what they feel. They are highly intuitive. Da Vinci was a big believer in using both parts of the brain. He was a whole-brain thinker. He showed this in his

notebooks by tying ideas with drawings. Specifically, he was the original mind-mapper.

6. **Cultivation of grace:** He was of the view that the cultivation of grace, ambidexterity, fitness, and poise are important for the growth of mental faculties. Therefore, he was inclined towards athletics apart from his mental prowess. He strongly believed that if he wanted his mind to perform at optimum levels, he needed to keep his body in perfect shape as well.

7. **Systems thinking**: He had a strong recognition and appreciation for the connectedness of all phenomena--a concept known as systems thinking. Systems thinking is when you are able to take vast amounts of information and create routines, lists and organization. It also has to do with pattern recognition. Da Vinci believed that "Everything comes from everything, and everything is made out of everything, and everything returns into everything."

Use Mind-Mapping to Turbo Charges Your Thinking Abilities

Your mind travels way faster than you can even imagine because it's all about billions of neurons wiring and firing with each other every fraction of a second. The kind of connections this builds between different pieces of information in your memory and experience is super-fast and difficult to fathom. Wouldn't it be exciting to see how these connections look on paper and what inferences you can draw?

Mind-mapping is the technique in which you can see the interactions and connections happening between different thoughts in your brain. It's nothing but a visual diagram. A mind map is hierarchical and illustrates the relationship between different pieces of information.

While **journaling** (as explained later) is mainly writing your thoughts in words to clear your head so you can process information better, **mind mapping** is used for decision making and problem solving when you want to list out and explore holistically all the related aspects of any problem.

It often begins with a central idea and then branches out into interconnected ideas related to that topic that can be shown as words or images. If you want to analyze various factors of a problem, mind mapping helps you see the different elements together in a holistic manner to analyze the bigger picture.

For example, say you want to start a new business. It will be in the center of your page, and from there you will branch out into connected ideas like which product, industry segment, targeted customer, competitors and the finance required, any partners, time period, pricing, marketing, and other key challenges, etc.

Mind mapping works on the principle that our minds are not ordered linearly. You had already done an experiment in the initial section of this book on how thoughts originate and keep traveling in any direction, if you let them flow. Mind mapping is taking benefit of this nonlinear way our minds work.

Mind mapping makes you a balanced thinker. On one sheet of paper, you start to see all your thoughts, i.e. your areas of concern based on past experience, as well as how your imagination creates new solutions. Mind mapping can be equated to a marriage between logic and imagination. Our left brain creates logical, rational thought processes based on the crystallized intelligence we have gained over years. On the other hand, our right brain uses imagery and colors and is creative and imagination oriented. When you start building a mind map, you are employing whole-brain thinking by capturing your logic as well as imagination on a piece of paper.

You can create mind maps of all sorts. It could be about a career move, your next vacation, making choices amongst two different items, or planning for a perfect dinner party with friends.

How do you do it?

All you need to start is a topic, some colored pens and a sheet of paper, and follow these rules.

- Begin with a symbol or picture representing your topic in the center
- Write key words or draw images on curved branches radiating from the center.
- Write one key word per line.
- Free associate and add smaller branches with images or words related to your key words.
- Use colors, pictures, dimensions and codes for greater association and emphasis.

I've used mind-mapping many times including outlining my books to counter the overwhelm of multiple ideas floating in my mind. You can use mind-mapping for any of your real-life situations, where you have to take into account multiple factors that are inter-connected. By preparing a mind-map, you'll be putting your logic and calculations as well ideas and imaginations about the situation, and thus will be using your left and right hemisphere, thus doing the whole-brain thinking and finding better solutions to your problems.

Chapter 6: Activate Your Physiology to Change the Way You Think

****

"To move the world, we must first move ourselves."

~ Socrates

Claim Your Power Hour

There is a saying, "Well begun is half done." Also, you know well that if you nurture your child in the initial years, he or she will grow into a good human being. The same applies to your days. If you begin your day well, you are significantly done.

"Lose an hour in the morning, and you will spend all day looking for it." ~Richard Whately

If you examine the life of great people, you'll find a pattern in their routines. They safeguard their mornings like the most treasured asset. The morning hour needs to be primed for solidifying the foundation of a great day, of which you can feel proud.

Mornings are sacred for a couple of reasons. You're up after a full night's refreshing sleep and your jelly-like brain is now pretty settled. It is not yet influenced by outside stimulants from your environment. Also, your mind is at the most creative stage at this point in time to think about and plan the important activities of the day.

Most people immediately disturb this most resourceful state of mind by picking up their smart phones. Without realizing it, within a few minutes of waking up, they have already started scrolling their emails, checking their social media feeds and all messages, and now all their thoughts and emotions have been distracted by outside stimulants. They have already given up their power.

But if you want to get results that only less than 1% people in the world achieve, you have to start differently. You need to make your first morning hour a power hour. This power hour should include certain important habits that will pave the way for an intelligent brain and help you think smarter and better throughout the day. A few activities are scientifically proven to improve your mental capabilities and make you a better thinker.

Move Your Body Change Your Brian

Although thinking is a cognitive function, our physiology and mental health plays a vital role in nurturing our thinking process. In the previous sections, we learned about how our thinking process works, the common thinking errors, and the best ways to start thinking effectively.

But knowing about something will not yield results; it's the implementation of that knowledge that will make you change your behavior and action, which in turn will produce results in life. That's why they say that knowledge is only the *potential* power; the real power lies in implementation.

Therefore, this section is dedicated to a discussion of how you can really implement that knowledge into your life by fine-tuning your body and mind by applying a universal principle. Using your body and mind effectively will do the job of smoothing the transition from your older and probably self-sabotaging patterns to a newer and more intelligent way of thinking. With principles that are research backed and used by the great thinkers of all time, you can implement the advanced strategies you learned so far in this book.

Let's start with the body. As you know, the brain is different from the mind; it's very much a physical organ like other organs of the body. Therefore, the efficient working of this organ depends on the optimal functioning of the entire body.

Our brain weighs just 2% of our total body weight, but it consumes more that 20% of our energy requirement. This is because the brain is responsible for managing all the body functions and movements, and giving directions to other organs through a variety of neuron signals. It is responsible for your entire thinking, decision making and memory processes, and maintains your repertoire of past instances and behaviors to make future life decisions. It's job is to keep you protected and safeguarded from danger and thus keeps you alive.

To carry out all these functions, the brain needs more energy than other body organs that have limited functions. This energy requirement is met by an efficient supply of blood and oxygen. The heart plays a vital role in the energy process through the rich supply of blood. In order to discharge its function effectively, the heart needs to be vibrant and healthy. To make our hearts healthy, we need to do regular exercise.

Unfortunately, the heart can't exercise on its own, as it is hidden deep inside the body layers. The exercise it needs is to increase the heart beat from its normal rate to a significantly higher rate, which varies depending upon age. To ensure that our heart functions robustly, it needs to be stressed and stretched beyond its regular heart beat rate.

It is estimated that if the heart beats more than its regular rate for 30 minutes a day regularly, then it will produce good results by way of an enhanced supply of blood and thus oxygen to the entire body, including the brain.

But how do you do the exercise the heart?

It's through the legs only. You either run or jog or do some other kind of cardiovascular exercises that brings your heart to the state of beating faster than its normal pace. Here is how you should meet the exercise requirement of your heart. Take 220 heart beats as a standard parameter and then subtract your age from this number. Whatever number comes up, you have to multiply your heart beat by at least 60% of that number. For example, if you are 30 years old, you should take your heart beat to 114 heart beats per minute (60% of 190 (220-30)) doing good exercise for around 30 minutes a day.

Generally, a good exercise regime increases your heart beat to around 80-85% of that number, which is a good sign of a healthy heart. The above is a rule of thumb for a normal person. However, if you are suffering from a heart specific problem, please consult your doctor or other health professional before adding any extreme exercise to your life.

A regular dose of exercise has magical effects on your brain and your thinking abilities. John Ratey in his book, Spark: *The Revolutionary New Science of Exercise and Brain,* states that exercise is truly our best defense against everything from depression to ADD to addiction to menopause to Alzheimer's. Rates explores comprehensively the connection between exercise and the brain:

Physical activity sparks biological changes that encourage brain cells to bind to one another. For the brain to learn, these connections must be made; they reflect the brain's fundamental ability to adapt to challenges. The more neuroscientists discover about this process, the clearer it becomes that exercise provides an unparalleled stimulus, creating an environment in which the brain is ready, willing, and able to learn.

A regular exercise regime stimulates the release of positive neurotransmitters, like dopamine (which encourages motivation, attention, and pleasure), serotonin (which enhances learning, mood, and self-esteem), and norepinephrine (which leads to arousal and alertness). The best part of Ratey's theory is that exercise expedites the production of BDNF (brain-derived neurotrophic factor), a protein which he has dubbed "Miracle-Gro for the brain."

Scientists have discovered an "exercise hormone" called *irisin* that is also linked to improved health and cognitive function. The part of the brain that responds strongly to aerobic exercise is the hippocampus. Experiments have been conducted showing that the structure of hippocampus increases once you get physically fit. Since the hippocampus is at the core of the brain's learning and memory systems, it enjoys the memory-boosting effects of cardiovascular fitness.[13]

Furthermore, Michael Gelb in *Think Like Leonardo Da Vinci* explains that with a few exceptions, the great geniuses of history were gifted with remarkable physical energy and aptitude. And it makes a common sense too. Seriously. How can you think of getting the best out of life, if you find it difficult to get out of bed?

Now let' move to next important aspect related to our body that helps to think clearer and better.

Rest and Rejuvenate Your Body

There is enough research now to establish that if you consistently compromise and deprive yourself of the required number of sleep hours every night, you may already be

[13] https://www.psychologytoday.com/blog/the-athletes-way/201404/physical-activity-improves-cognitive-function

in the grip of stress and anxiety. Sleep deprivation studies repeatedly show a variable (negative) impact on mood, cognitive performance, and motor function due to an increasing destabilization of the waking state. Specific neurocognitive domains, including executive attention, working memory, and divergent higher cognitive functions are particularly vulnerable to sleep loss.

Lack of sleep saps willpower because if you are sleep deprived, your cells have trouble absorbing glucose from the bloodstream. A lack of glucose makes the body under-fueled and exhausted. In a state of fatigue, the brain wants to conserve energy for the body's normal operations. As there is low stock of energy, the brain has to retain enough for any emergency situation. You can imagine how difficult it would be for our brains to effectively learn and implement a newer approach to thinking in such a situation, and therefore it takes the easiest route--using the preset pattern of thinking as a means of conserving energy.

The prefrontal cortex is responsible for executive functions like focus, memory, and making decisions; suffers most due to the lack of energy caused by sleep deprivation. The studies also suggest that sleep loss produces temporary changes in cerebral metabolism, cognition, emotion, and behavior that is something equivalent to mild prefrontal dysfunction.[14]

If you are truly sincere about harnessing the true potential of your brain and developing cognitive abilities like the great thinkers, you need to ensure that you get the right quantity and quality of sleep every night. The National Sleep Foundation in a study about sleep time duration came out with specific recommendations about the minimum number of hours of sleep required for people of different age groups. The study panel agreed that for healthy individuals getting normal sleep, the appropriate sleep duration should be 7 to 9 hours for young adults and adults and between 7 to 8 hours for older adults.

The key point to emphasize here is that if you take care of your body by consuming nutritious diet, exercising well and sleeping adequate number of hours, this is like building the right infrastructure for thinking clearer. Just by taking care of your body

[14] https://www.ncbi.nlm.nih.gov/pubmed/17765011

properly, you'll see a enhanced clarity in your thinking approach, you'll see rise in your creativity, ideas will seem naturally coming to you at times you least expect.

However, if you take additional care of your mental aspects in addition to your body, you'll create a more robust infrastructure, because all thinking happens in your mind only. Therefore, let's move to the last section of this book, where we will discuss about some mental techniques and how they can help you think intelligently.

Chapter 7: Mental Tools to Transform Your Thinking

****

"To do much clear thinking a person must arrange for regular periods of solitude when they can concentrate and indulge the imagination without distraction."

~ Thomas A. Edison

In the previous chapter, we learned about how working on our bodies can provide immense benefits. Exercise sharpens our brain's physical structure by increasing the blood and oxygen flow. We can think much more clearly.

But don't stop at the physical level only. Physical exercise is good and helpful; but that's only a good starting point of the game of intelligent thinking. You pave the way to better thinking by getting physically fit, but you also need to exercise your mental faculties. In this section, we will learn a couple of mental Tools that can help you think better and clearer.

Journaling

Did you know that Bill Gates paid 30.8 million US dollars for 18 sheets of journaling by Leonardo Da Vinci?

Isn't it surprising?

What was so precious about those few pieces of papers that made Gates pay this huge sum of money?

Gates knew that Da Vinci's mind was filled with diagrams, sketches and a lot of iterations of ideas. By looking at these images, he could understand the thinking process of the genius. Through these pages, Gates wanted to get a glimpse inside Da Vinci's mind. Here is a sample of what Da Vinci's journal looked like.

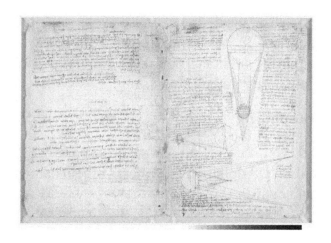

(image source[15]: Business Insider[16]

Great people do journaling, as they want to see physically what's going on in their heads. You can't objectively assess them if you let your thoughts wander aimlessly. Journaling helps you see your thoughts as physical objects. It's a mechanism of self-awareness and you know it well by now that the first step to change is awareness. Journaling helps you see and then edit your thinking process. Once you see what's going on in your head on paper, you start improving the

---

quality of your thoughts, as you proceed to the next level.

Great minds write in their journals almost every day. Leonardo penned 7,000 pages of intense notes in his. In fact, journaling is a self-coaching mechanism. Though, it can't replace coaching, but it can offer you some benefits of a coach. How? Let's understand what a coach does for you.

A coach doesn't always need to give you expert advice. Most of the time, his or her job is to help you process what's going on in your head. In most coaching sessions, people tend to get "aha" moments, while simply exposing their internal thinking process to their coaches. The answers come naturally to them.

Journaling is simply writing your thoughts, emotions and feelings to clear your mind, and it's particularly good for liberating yourself from self-limiting beliefs. It's recommended to do it daily. I know that a few of my mentors do journaling both every morning and evening. I've been doing morning journaling for many years, and now I have started doing evening journals too. While the morning journal helps put you into right state of mind by noting your mini or major accomplishments of the previous day, it also makes you feel grateful and is a reminder to plan for the day. On the other hand, evening journaling helps you to reflect on how the day went. What did you learn during the day? Did you become better than yesterday? Is there any feedback or area of improvement to be done the next day, etc.

What do you write in the journal?

I had tried bullet point style journaling that I learned from Hal Elrod's book, Miracle Morning, which I found very useful. It was specifically jotting down details about a few specific areas. Here is how it worked:

- What are you grateful for?
- What was your key achievement? You must have done at least something to move further towards your goal. Jot it down.
- Any specific areas of improvement.
- What needs to be done today that will make you feel like you are winning.

If you haven't yet started a journal yet, you should take your first step and spend a few minutes getting your thinking on paper.

You'll see an improvement in self-awareness, notice the free space in your head and eventually get more clarity in the thinking process. You can get started with by answering the specific questions as listed above.

Needless to mention, mornings are the best time to write in your journal and capture the fresh thoughts of the morning and plan your day. You'll realize a lighter mind that will attract more ideas and will make you a smart thinker.

Mindfulness Strengthens Your Brain

The next important mental exercise is mindfulness. You can see your body exercising, because it is tangible and anyone from the outside can directly see it happening. But mindfulness is an inner exercise that only you can see to perfect your moves.

Mindfulness is no longer considered as mediation by monks sitting in caves. It's very much a part of business and boardrooms today. Given the benefits mindfulness, big companies like Google, Facebook, and even government departments, prisons and schools in the US have adopted it open-heartedly. There are frequent mindfulness meditation sessions being conducted in the corporate world and in general.

Mindfulness has become quite a mainstream thing in recent few decades because of the well-researched and widely-known benefits it offers to people doing meditation. In her book, *The Willpower Instinct: How Self-Control Works, Why It Matters, and What You Can Do To Get More of It,* author Kelly McGonigal, psychologist and researcher, describes the benefits of meditation.

> *Neuroscientists have now found that when we make ourselves sit and instruct our brain to meditate, not only it gets better at meditating, but it develops a wide range of self-control skills, including attention, focus, stress management, impulse control, and self-awareness. Science tells that people who meditate regularly for longer periods, have more gray matter in the prefrontal cortex, as well as other regions of the brain that support self-awareness.*

Another study found that eight weeks of daily meditation practice lead to increased self-awareness in everyday life, as well as increased gray matter in corresponding areas of the brain. It may seem incredible that our brains can reshape themselves so quickly, but meditation increases blood flow to the prefrontal cortex in much the same way that lifting weights increases blood flow to muscles. The brain appears to adapt to exercise in the same way that muscles do, getting both bigger and faster in order to get better at what you ask of them.

How do you do mindfulness?

There is no specific pose or asana that is must for mindfulness. You can do it anywhere while sitting, walking, mowing the lawn, or doing the dishes. The only thing you need to do is focus on your breath coming in and going out. Start with 10 minutes a day.

It's better if you dedicate yourself to sitting in silence without moving your body to help you get much deeper and give you better benefits. Mindfulness meditation expert, Sam Harris, compares doing meditation tp walking on a rope; it easy to explain but difficult to master, but then he goes on to describe the steps needed for mindfulness practice[17].

1. Sit comfortably with your spine erect, either in a chair or cross-legged on a cushion.

2. Close your eyes, take a few deep breaths, and feel the points of contact between your body and the chair or floor. Notice the sensations associated with sitting—feelings of pressure, warmth, tingling, vibration, etc.

3. Gradually become aware of the process of breathing. Pay attention to wherever you feel your breath most clearly—either at the nostrils or in the rising and falling of your abdomen.

4. Allow your attention to rest in the mere sensation of breathing. (There is no need to control your breath. Just let it come and go naturally.)

5. Every time your mind wanders, gently return it to the sensation of breathing.

6. As you focus on your breath, you will notice that other perceptions and sensations continue to appear:

_____

sounds, feelings in your body, emotions, etc. Simply notice these phenomena as they emerge into the field of awareness and then return to the sensation of breathing.

7. The moment you observe that you have been lost in thought, notice the present thought itself as an object of consciousness. Then return your attention to the breath—or to whatever sounds or sensations arise in the next moment.

8. Continue in this way until you have witnessed all objects of consciousness—sights, sounds, sensations, emotions, and even thoughts themselves—as they arise and pass away.

9. Don't fall.

Those who are new to the practice generally find it useful to hear instructions poken aloud in the form of a guided meditation." There are plenty of guided meditation apps[18] available these days that can help you to do a guided meditation.

---

[18] http://sombathla.com/stressfree

In addition to formal seated practice, we can also bring in the practice of mindfulness during our daily activities: while eating, walking, and talking. For meditation practice in daily life, the idea is to pay attention to what is going on in the present moment and to be aware of what is happening – and not live unconsciously. If you are eating, it means paying attention to the food you are eating--its smell, how you chew it, and how you swallow the food. If you are walking, it means being more aware of your body movements, your feet touching the ground, the sounds you are hearing, etc. For more information, you can refer to my book on mindfulness *The Mindful Mind*.

I know everybody is busy – life is too demanding. There doesn't appear any time left to add even a single activity in your life. Therefore I don't want you to burden with too much stuff to be incorporated in your already jam-packed life.

But please note that the physical and mental aspects stated in last two sections can be compared like putting gas into your vehicle. You can't fool yourself that you can drive faster and reach sooner at your destination, when you know that you vehicle is short of fuel.

Therefore, if you are serious about thinking clearly and intelligently, all the techniques stated in earlier sections will definitely and immensely help you, but if you add these minimal amount of physical and mental activities, as stated in the last two sections of these book, that will be really an icing on the cake, I promise.

Conclusion

****

The most important investment you can make is in yourself."

~ Warren Buffett

Congratulations!

You made it till the end. I sincerely hope you are thinking and feeling wiser than your prior self. We started this whole journey by understanding our thinking process, its flaws, and how we can change our thinking process. Then we moved on to understand the various approaches to changing our thinking, and finally we examined how to implement newer strategies by priming our bodies and minds through the right techniques.

As mentioned earlier, mere knowledge is not power; it's *potential* power. It's the implementation of knowledge that gives you real power. And the best part is that the implementation of the lessons learned in this book are not difficult to apply in everyday life. Every moment you are thinking something, you always have the opportunity to experiment with different approaches.

You can immediately start by looking at your cognitive biases. The next time you go shopping, you'll start to see the anchoring bias. Similarly, when you face your next problem, you can quickly start to think from first principle thinking, going on to deconstructing the problem and seeing its various constituents minutely. You're now aware of integrative thinking and can start taking into account the multiple aspects of different interconnected parameters and get to a solution that holistically addresses all the aspects.

You have lot of stuff to practice and implement in your day-to-day routine. You also understand that to significantly improve the quality of your thinking, you will need to develop some resourceful habits by fine-tuning your body and mind.

In a nutshell, you have now equipped yourself with the wisdom needed to improve the quality of your thinking to transform your decisions and thus the quality of your life.

I hope you'll put the advice compiled in this book into your actions. I would be very happy to know if and how these thoughts have helped you transform your life in any manner.

Wishing you nothing but a life of wisdom and joy,

Cheers

May I ask you for a small favor?

At the outset, I want to give you a big thanks for taking out time to read this book. You could have chosen any other book, but you took mine, and I totally appreciate this.

I hope you got at least a few actionable insights that will have a positive impact on your day to day life.

Can I ask for 30 seconds more of your time?

I'd love if you could leave a review about the book. Reviews may not matter to big-name authors; but they're a tremendous help for authors like me, who don't have much following. They help me to grow my readership by encouraging folks to take a chance on my books.

To put it straight– **reviews are the life blood for any author.**

Please leave your review by clicking below link, it will directly lead you to book review page.

DIRECT REVIEW LINK FOR "INTELLIGENT THINKING"

It will just take less than a minute of your time, but will tremendously help me to reach out to more people, so please leave your review.

Thanks for your support to my work. And I'd love to see your review.

Preview of the book "Think Out of the Box"

Chapter 1: Introduction

****

"Instead of thinking outside the box, get rid of the box."

— Deepak Chopra

An Out of the Box Story

Once, there was a poor farmer who lived with his daughter in a village. He owed a huge debt to the village head. He was working hard to earn and repay his debt by way of smaller installments every month. But despite that, the debt amount was getting bigger and bigger instead of being reduced, as the rate of interest charged by the village head was exorbitantly high.

This village head was not only greedy, but he had evil intentions. He wanted to marry the farmer's beautiful daughter, who was less than half of his age. He also knew that the burgeoning amount of loan had already put the farmer in a state of anxiety and depression, as the farmer was not only worried about putting food on the table daily, his topmost concern was his daughter's marriage and to provide for her better future.

Knowing all that, the village head thought of exploiting the farmer's unfortunate situation and proposed him with an offer that could alleviate all the problems of the farmer once and for all. He offered to forego the farmer's entire debt and interest, if his daughter would agree to play one game. In the game, there was a non-transparent steel jar that would contain two pebbles in it – one black and the other white. The farmer's daughter just needed to put her hand in the jar with closed eyes and pick out one of the pebbles from a jar without looking inside.

Here were the conditions of the game:

    a. If she picked a black pebble, the debt would be forgiven.

    b. However, if she picks a white pebble, the debt would still be forgiven but she had to marry that village head.

The farmer was hesitant and skeptical of the intentions of the village head, as he didn't want to put her daughter's life in jeopardy by letting her marry the wicked village head. But his daughter somehow convinced him to play the game, as she wanted to sincerely help her father get rid of all his financial woes. Moreover, there was still a 50% chance for her to win, i.e. waiver of the loan without marrying the village head.

Next day, the farmer, his daughter, the village head, and some other villagers went to gravel (a piece of land covered with pebbles). A random villager was asked to quickly pick two pebbles (one black, one white) and put them in the jar.

But as you might have guessed, how could the village head, being so greedy and wicked, have such a big offer to waive the loan solely on 50% probability and lose his money without getting married to the farmer's daughter. In fact, the evil village head had already bribed that stranger to somehow secretly ensure that he put both white pebbles in the jar. However, since her entire life was on stake, while nobody else could notice, the farmer's daughter observed this mischief.

Now for a moment, assume you are there in her situation. What will you do?

There seem to be only two options:

Alternative 1: Don't say anything, pick up one of the white pebbles, lose the game, and marry the evil guy.

Alternative 2: Publicly reveal that the jar has two white pebbles.

She obviously didn't want to marry him, so option 1 was not the preferred choice. But she wanted to definitely help her father by getting his loan forgiven so that both she and her father could lead a better life. But she also knew that if she opted for option 2, then the village head would get annoyed and make their life more miserable.

She was in a fix, but then she thought for a moment and went ahead.

Following the rules of the game, she picked up one pebble from the jar. But before showing it to anyone she dropped it in the gravel in a way that it seemed like a mistake. Fortunately, since the gravel was all covered with mixed white and black pebbles, no one could tell which one she picked.

She apologized for her mistake, but smartly suggested that if some villagers could check the other pebble remaining in the jar, it could then be determined easily which pebble she had picked. There was no reason to disagree with the daughter's suggestion, so the village head had to agree.

It seemed so natural to everyone when the villager picked out a white pebble from the jar. Therefore it meant that the girl had picked the black pebble.

Therefore, following the rules of the game, picking up black pebble entitled the girl to get the loan of her father waived without getting married to the village head. The village head guy was bewildered and got frustrated but couldn't say anything because she won fair and square, as it appeared on the face of it.

Here the girl played the smart game secretly out-of-the-jar by following the out-of the-box thinking approach.

You see how the girl created a third option, while there were seemingly only two options.

For a moment, assume even if she had called out that the game was unfair, the stranger could have said he did it by mistake, and he would pick two pebbles again and put them in the jar. But even in that option she would still run a 50% chance of losing. The option she took was not obvious to anyone but it guaranteed her win by taking advantage of the rigged game. By out of the box thinking, she created 100% secure option that made her help her father as well as safeguard herself from getting into the trap of the evil village head.

I read this story somewhere. I'm not sure if this is true or merely a work of fiction, but obviously it isn't so imaginative and unreal like the time travel scenes you see in the sci-fi movies. Regardless of the fact of whether the story was fictional or true instance, there is a real message that resonates 100% when it comes to looking at the different alternatives in our lives.

Do we only look at the limited visible options for solving any problem or do we use our brain to generate some novel and unique thoughts that open up newer and unforeseen alternatives, which can put us on the faster track to solve our problems in a better manner?

In most of the cases, we don't go beyond what is obvious and therefore limit ourselves to only those available options that everyone else sees. Consequently, such option is bound to give mediocre results, as everybody would follow suit.

For a moment, imagine how your life would be, if you could generate thoughts and ideas that others are not able to see. Wouldn't it transform the way you make choices and thus get better results?

Obviously, this would immensely improve your confidence and thus the quality of your life.

Before we move ahead, let's get some more flavor of how thinking out of the box operates by looking at some real-world examples, where out of the box thinking approach transformed many businesses.

Real-world Out of the Box Examples

For the first example, let me ask you what comes to your mind instantly when you hear the name, Philips.

Even today, for most people, Philips is a brand name that is synonymous with electronic equipment like television, music or sound system and related stuff. Of course, Philips started with electronics, but today, the majority percentage of revenue of Philips is contributed by an altogether different product line i.e. healthcare products.

Currently, healthcare products are the major contributors to the top line and the bottom line of Philips. Some might wonder how an electronic home appliance company ventured out in a totally different industry of manufacturing medical equipment and garnered so much profitability that it exceeded the sales and profits of its initial product line, i.e., electronics?

It definitely was out of the box thinking approach to transition from one product model to an entirely different range of unrelated product segment. Producing a microwave oven versus producing an incubator for a new born baby although both of them are machines, but till the time Philips thought within the box of home appliances, no one could think of getting into healthcare products.

It was only when they realized that the technology used in manufacturing home appliance could be applied to producing healthcare products by meeting certain different specifications. It was this out of the box thinking that made them transition into an entirely new business vertical.

Let's take another example.

BIC, a French company initially started with all kinds of writing products, i.e., pencils and other stationery products like ballpoint pens, markers, colors etc. But later on, they shifted from paper products to other unrelated products vis-à-vis stationery items. They started producing razors, lighters, perfumes, etc.

What made them expand to another unrelated type of product line?

In fact, they thought of their existing business in an altogether different way. While they initially believed that their business was just about creating writing products, here, the company adopted an out of the box thinking approach. They realized that their business could be categorized as a business of manufacturing disposable items. Once they thought about their business from this new lens, anything that could be disposed of became their business model, hence manufacturing lighters, razors, perfumes etc. was not something that they could ignore further.

What it took was thinking out of the box from "writing products" to "disposable products." And that made them expand in different verticals.

Let's take one example from the world of sports. For a moment, if you think of athletes before Roger Bannister, a British athlete, they never thought that running one mile in less than 4 minutes was even humanly possible. Even the coaches of Roger Bannister mocked him off at first when Roger apprised them about him taking a challenge of running a mile in less than 4 minutes. But on May 6, 1954, Roger Bannister with unconventional thinking clubbed with dedication and commitment proved that the old belief about human impossibility of running a mile in less than 4 minutes was a limited in-the-box-thinking approach only.

Today, you see out of the box thinking happening all around at such a rapid pace leading to massive technological development and innovation. If you look around, you'll see so many creative ideas taking shape that just two generations ago would have appeared like some hypothetical science fiction story.

Imagine the pace of evolution of humans from the time when people used to think that the earth was at the center of the universe (and the sun was rotating around the earth in orbits) to a realization, where we are thinking not only about space travel, but also developing space tourism– thanks to out of the box thinkers like Elon Musk and Richard Branson. Hundreds of people including Ashton Kutcher, Leonardo DiCaprio, and Justin Bieber already placed a deposit for space travel for USD 250,000 for *Unity* Spacecraft, a Richard Branson's space travel initiative.

Today, a small robot (with artificial intelligence) can do so many tasks for you from selecting music, switching our lights on or off or making calls for you – think about Alexa (from Amazon).

What do all these stories talk about?

They only exemplify the role of creative or innovating thinking or what we often term as thinking out of the box and how it has transformed human experience so far and will continue to do so.

What This Book Can Do For You?

Of course, we can go on and on with so many real-life stories of innovation and out of box thinking that this book can be titled "Thinking out of the Box Stories."

But I know that you don't want only that. You want to know how you can get started with out of the box thinking in your life, to solve your problems and achieve your goals. You want to know how you can develop your cognitive abilities, so you could generate more creative ideas and gain an edge over others in terms of providing solutions.

This book will change how you perceive your creativity, while stripping creativity itself of its mystique. If you are able to generate ideas that deliver results, it has the potential to shift the trajectory of your life.

You will perhaps start seeing endless possibilities stretching before you. You will learn how to:

- Generate ideas on demand.
- Find new ways to make money.
- Create new business opportunities.
- Manipulate and modify existing ideas to make them powerful.
- Create new products, services, and processes.
- Develop solutions to complex business problems.

- See problems as opportunities.
- Become more productive.
- Be the "idea person" in your organization.
- Know where to look for the "breakthrough idea."

Above is just to list a few benefits.

I want to equip you with the most effective strategies that will help you think out of the box and help you get creative ideas on demand. I know it's a big promise, but here is the thing. The strategies I'm telling in the book are not something invented by me, rather they are used by the many creative thinkers of the world. Since they have worked for them, it should work for you and me as well (yes, I'm on the same journey).

Out of the Box Thinking is for anyone and everyone.

Don't think that generating creative ideas is something that is reserved only for some artistic personalities like painters, writers, musicians, or some other creative tribe. Also, don't misunderstand that out-of-the-box thinking is only for superbly talented entrepreneurs who want to put a dent in the world.

Don't set yourself into some secluded category and limit yourself for a conventional path that delivers just mediocre results. Creative thinking is for anyone who wants to think and act differently from the standard way of doing things. Thinking of different ways of arriving at best solutions by spending lesser time, money, and energy is and should be the objective of every growth-oriented individual.

--End of Preview--

Get your copy of the full book >>> _Think Out of The Box_

Other Books in <u>Power-Up Your Brain Series</u>

1. ***Intelligent Thinking:*** *Overcome Thinking Errors, Learn Advanced Techniques to Think Intelligently, Make Smarter Choices, and Become the Best Version of Yourself (Power-Up Your Brain Series Book 1)*

2. ***Think Out of The Box:*** *Generate Ideas on Demand, Improve Problem Solving, Make Better Decisions, and Start Thinking Your Way to the Top (Power-Up Your Brain Series Book 2)*

3. ***Make Smart Choices:*** *Learn How to Think Clearly, Beat Information Anxiety, Improve Decision Making Skills, and Solve Problems Faster (Power-Up Your Brain Series Book 3)*

4. *__Build A Happier Brain:__* *The Neuroscience and Psychology of Happiness. Learn Simple Yet Effective Habits for Happiness in Personal, Professional Life and Relationships (Power-Up Your Brain Book 4)*

5. *__Think With Full Brain:__* *Strengthen Logical Analysis, Invite Breakthrough Ideas, Level-up Interpersonal Intelligence, and Unleash Your Brain's Full Potential (Power-Up Your Brain Series Book 5)*

Printed in Great Britain
by Amazon

30314593R00098